about teany:

"I can happily report that meat eaters will not feel like they are partaking of rabbit food."
—*The Village Voice*

"Teany features a delicious gourmet menu."
—*Time Out*

"A great American food find."
—*The Food Network*

"Moby: guitars, synthesizers, film scores, a restaurant (an oasis for the vegetarian on the Lower East Side), a beverage-distribution empire, and now culinary literature. In each case, there are fireworks of the passionate demiurge."
—*Rick Moody, author of* <u>*The Ice Storm*</u>

"I love Teany. When we were rehearsing one of my films around the corner, we ate there every day."
—*John Cameron Mitchell, writer/director of* <u>*Hedwig and the Angry Inch*</u>

teany book

teany book

stories, food, romance, cartoons, and, of course, tea

Moby and Kelly Tisdale

Viking Studio

VIKING STUDIO
Published by the Penguin Group
Penguin Group (USA) Inc., 375 Hudson Street,
New York, New York 10014, U.S.A.
Penguin Group (Canada), 10 Alcorn Avenue,
Toronto, Ontario, Canada M4V 3B2
(a division of Pearson Penguin Canada Inc.)
Penguin Books Ltd, 80 Strand, London WC2R 0RL, England
Penguin Ireland, 25 St. Stephen's Green, Dublin 2, Ireland
(a division of Penguin Books Ltd)
Penguin Books Australia Ltd, 250 Camberwell Road,
Camberwell, Victoria 3124, Australia (a division of Pearson Australia Group Pty Ltd)
Penguin Books India Pvt Ltd, 11 Community Centre,
Panchsheel Park, New Delhi – 110 017, India
Penguin Group (NZ), Cnr Airborne and Rosedale Roads, Albany,
Auckland 1310, New Zealand (a division of Pearson New Zealand Ltd)
Penguin Books (South Africa) (Pty) Ltd, 24 Sturdee Avenue,
Rosebank, Johannesburg 2196, South Africa

Penguin Books Ltd, Registered Offices:
80 Strand, London WC2R 0RL, England

First published in 2005 by Viking Studio,
a member of Penguin Group (USA) Inc.

1 2 3 4 5 6 7 8 9 10

Text copyright © Richard Melville Hall and Kelly Tisdale, 2005
All rights reserved

CIP data available
ISBN 1-42-00505-3
Printed in China
Set in Helvetica Neue T1

Book Design by Elanna Allen
Illustrations by Moby and Elanna Allen
Food photography by Paul Johnson
Food styling by Michael di Beneditto
Other interior photography by Moby, Elanna Allen, Irina Lazar, and Chris Cruz

This book (or the half that I wrote) is dedicated to my parents and Moby.
—Kelly

This book (or the half that I wrote) is dedicated to Kelly and her dog, Pineapple.
—Moby

Awe, that's nice. Thanks, Moby.
—Kelly

Hey, no problem. And thanks for dedicating your half, or technically
quarter, to me!
—Moby

But wait. Don't you think that we should also dedicate a part of our
book to our lovely teany customers and the nice neighborhood
people that have been so great to us since we opened?
—Kelly

Yes, Kelly, you're absolutely right.
—Moby

We also dedicate two-fifths of this book to our wonderful teany customers
and neighbors.
—Kelly and Moby

Contents

foreword

by David Cross

Hello. My name is Olin Stubing and I am the owner of Olin's Gas-Powered Rider-Mower Warehouse. I am an avid outdoorsman who lifts weights in the name of Jesus. I live in Winsbrook, Michigan, with my wife, Donna, and our two boys, Peter and Luke. I received a copy of this book in the mail with the request to write a foreword to it. I believe it was sent to the wrong address because my name is not David Cross; it's Olin.

I am not a vegetarian. I am a vociferous meat eater (I've won my own made-up barbecue tournaments in my head several times), I rarely drink tea, and I am not very familiar with much contemporary rock music. I know very little of Moby's work. He did that one song for that car ad on TV, is that right? Anyway, I am definitely a meat and potatoes kind of guy as opposed to a sun-dried tomato and white bean spread and fresh tomato sandwich (page 19) kind of guy.

I see that part of this book starts with this Moby sitting in a bed thinking it would be nice to own a little vegetarian tea shop. Well, sir, I've never ever thought such a thought in my life. I'm sure I don't know anybody who has, either. Sometimes I'll have a glass of iced tea if it's hot out and I've run out of Hamms, but I just can't imagine—hang on, there's the phone and I've got to get it. Donna's out at her Tuesday-night ladies bee and the boys are in youth camp learning how to hunt and kill Indians like in the old days (not for real—it's all an act), so I'm sitting here by myself so I've got to get—oh, wait, it stopped. That's good. Anyhoo, as I was saying, I don't know about tea or tea shops or tea-shop men. Anything other than iced tea makes me nervous and I—now there's that darned phone again, hold on. Hey now! That was the editor of the book that this foreword is for. They did send it to the wrong address! But seeing as how they have a deadline to get this in by, they just want me to send in what I've written. So, here you go:

Teany has been described as a "Zen delight" by those who know (*Entertainment Weekly*) what a Zen delight truly is and can explain what the heck that really means. I would like to know what they mean by that, so *Entertainment Weekly*, please write me back. I read that Sophia Coppola, the wine guy's daughter, says that she enjoys sipping champagne on the terrace. I've seen a picture of that terrace and I couldn't fit no more than a Yamaha Powerblader 260-I on that thing if I set it sideways! Is that New York's idea of a terrace? No thank you. Let's see, there's recipes for European-sounding sandwiches in here . . . there's something about "facial steams," there's a thing about putting old, used teabags on your eyes if they're too puffy because you stayed up all night watching Johnny Depp movies. Huh? Once again, I am not gay or a misguided woman, so I guess this doesn't apply to me. There's all kinds of things of this nature, using tea for skin treatments, hair rinses, foot soaks, and the like.

In summation, I guess this book is good if you like all the things that I listed, like recipes for all kinds of vegetarian foods and various uses for tea that you haven't thought of and New York City history and pictures of Moby and his lady friend. But you probably like all those things because you bought the book already and that's why you're reading this now, huh? Well, good for you. If you ever come up to Winsbrook stop in if my wife is home and I'm not.

Thank you for your time I guess,

Olin

acknowledgments

Thanks to: Lulu for being so cute, Cathy (Lulu's mom) for letting her be cute in front of our camera, Dimitri for his lovely poem, Irina Lazar for her Asian salad wisdom, Maggie Burkle and Amanda Cohen for mixing tasty things in tofu cream cheese, Nelson Offley for helping us perfect our recipes, Nurse Carla for lending us her home, hallway, and outfits, Michael Beneditto for making our recipes look beautiful, Paul Johnson for taking pictures of Michael's food stylings, Elanna Allen for being a genius (and drawing, laying out, and designing our book), Maggie Long for being a design diva, David Vigliano for guiding us through the book publishing jungle, Chris Cruz for organizing all of our disorganization, Bill Thomas for our lovely cover portrait, Max Fish and all of the mental support it provided, and all of the nice people at Viking Studio, especially Kristen Jennings, for correcting all of our misspellings and making us look smarter than we really are.

Preface

For the last few months Kelly and I have been working on this teany book (that you are presently holding in your hands. Or so I assume. Maybe someone is reading this to you. Then you wouldn't be holding it in your hands. Or maybe you live in outer space where there is no gravity and the book is just floating in front of you. That would be cool.). And I've had the hardest time trying to describe the book to my friends.

"Is it a cookbook?" They ask.

"Well no," I reply. "It's not really a cookbook even though it does have a lot of nice recipes."

"Well, is it a book about you and Kelly?"

"Well, no," I reply. (And at this point my friends start to get frustrated. I mean who wants to be wrong two times in a row?) "Although, there are a lot of pictures of Kelly and me in the book, and we do talk about the fact that we have somehow figured out how to be ex-boyfriend/girlfriend and run a restaurant together and not kill each other."

"Okay," they finally ask. "What kind of book is it?" And then I give the annoyingly cryptic answer, "Well, it's a book about teany. It has tea and food and tea robots and a fake history of teany on the Lower East Side and lots of strange and interesting stories and anecdotes and cartoons and even some romance."

"Oh," my friends then say. "Why didn't you just say that to begin with?" To which I have no good answer, so I buy them a drink and ask them what their favorite *Simpsons* episode is. My favorite *Simpsons* episode (not that you're asking) is the little tree house of horrors with *The Shining* and where Homer goes back in time to the land of the dinosaurs. But I digress.

This is our teany book, and it's a bit hard to describe, but hopefully you'll enjoy reading it. And if there's a part of the book that you don't like, well, just flip around because there are a lot of different things in the book, and we presumptuously believe that you'll find something fun and interesting here.

Thanks,
Moby (and Kelly)

Chapter 1: Comrade Moby's Revisionist Prehistory of Teany

This chapter is, as the chapter title might suggest, my historical description of the facts and circumstances (loosely and subjectively presented) that led up to the opening of teany. The history ends with teany's opening night, because teany's history since then has been interesting but a bit tautological. And yes, *tautological* is a fantastic word, and I tend to repeat myself a lot so it's a good word for my friends to know so that they can sound erudite when they make fun of me for repeating myself ad nauseam.

the story of teany

In 1987, I spent a summer as a pretentious American on vacation in Paris with my girlfriend at the time, and after stumbling around some seemingly impressive museums, I found myself in a *salon de thé*. It was called La Bouillante, and even through the haze of my pretentiousness, I could see that it was a special little place.

I remember saying to my girlfriend at the time, "Wouldn't it be nice to own a little vegetarian tea shop?" I can't remember her answer, but it was probably something along the lines of, "You live in an abandoned factory in Stamford, Connecticut, and you bathe in a sink, and you're dreaming about opening a tea shop?"

But I was not deterred, and a mere fourteen years later, I was lying in bed with my girlfriend at the time, Kelly, as we both nursed terrible hangovers. Once again, I found myself mumbling, "Wouldn't it be nice to own a little vegetarian tea shop? It could serve, among other things, great hangover food and be in our own neighborhood."

To my delight, Kelly replied, "I, too, wish that there was a vegetarian tea shop that had great hangover food and that was in the neighborhood."

"Do you think that someday I will be paraphrasing this conversation in the interest of narrative exposition?" I asked.

"You are a pretentious jerk," she replied.

What made the idea seem even more appealing this time around (besides the fact that I now bathe in sinks by choice and not by necessity) was that we both had very similar thoughts about what this café should be like. We agreed that it should be local. (What's the point in owning a café if you can't hang out

there?) It should be vegetarian but should appeal to everyone (since Kelly is a vegetarian and I'm a vegan). It should be relaxed and comfortable, and we should have two tea robots as our mascots.

So after some more mumbling and moaning (not the good, sexy kind of moaning, but the I'm-full-of-hangover-germs kind of moaning), we decided that we would try to find a space in the neighborhood and open a vegetarian tea shop that would, among other things, serve great hangover food.

After our hungover discussion about possibly opening a vegetarian tea shop, Kelly and I actually decided to look around to see if there were any spaces in the neighborhood that might be appropriate homes for cute, vegetarian tea shops. Kelly started pounding the pavement and meeting with real estate agents. She looked at eighteen thousand storefronts (well, I might be exaggerating), and none of them were right. Some were too small, some were too expensive, some were too dark, some were too big, some were in the wrong neighborhood, and some smelled like pee.

But then one day we were walking around our neighborhood and we saw that the hair salon at 90 Rivington Street had closed and that the space was for rent. We looked at the space and saw that it was in the perfect location (i.e., where we both lived), faced south, had an outdoor space, and was cute and small.

We walked into the real-estate office and met with Bella, our real estate agent, and said, like excited six-year-olds, "We want the space! Please rent us the space! We'll do your dishes for you and wash your car! Please rent us the space!" Bella said that she would get our offer to the owner and then get back to us, which didn't suit my impatience at all, but I guess that's the way the real

Teany's opening night party pictures

world (as opposed to my self-involved, impulsive world) actually works. A few impatient weeks later, our offer was accepted!

Now we had to figure out how to renovate a space and set up a restaurant and deal with permits and contractors and architects and distributors and etc. Oh, and when I say "we" I do actually mean "Kelly" because she has invariably done all of the hard work while I just kind of hung out and ate cake.

Now that we had the lease signed, we took a moment to sit back and say, "Uh-oh." See, we had been so keen on finding the space and coming up with the concept that we hadn't really thought about what actually having a space and opening a restaurant might entail. I was considerably more sanguine about the impending process because, as I said earlier, I wasn't really going to be doing much of the work. At this point, I imagine that Kelly was having panic attacks and sleepless nights thinking, *What the hell have I gotten myself into?*

One of the first things that we had to do was to come up with a name. We had a long list with some good names (hers) and some bad names (mine). The list has since been burned. Or eaten. So I don't remember any of the bad names that I came up with, but I do remember that at the time I thought they were brilliant. Then Kelly suggested *teany*. And my initial reaction was: "I dunno. Shouldn't we name it after an animal, or something?" But then I thought about it and I realized that *teany* was a great name because a) we wanted to sell tea, b) we were in New York, and c) the space was very small. So we had a name: *teany*.

In the winter of 2001, Kelly was doing teany-related stuff like meeting with prospective architects. I'm not 100 percent sure what she was doing because I was quite busy finishing an album (*18*) and doing photo and video shoots. After finishing the album, my world consisted of the following: airplanes, hotels, and interviews. I can show you pictures from this period, and that's all that there is to it. I'm not complaining, but going from Los Angeles to New York to London to Munich to Madrid to Stockholm to Milan to Paris to Singapore to New Zealand to Brisbane to Sydney to Melbourne to Los Angeles to New York to London to Tokyo to etc. is tiring after a while. And I know that I'm getting off subject because I'm supposed to be writing about teany. But I wasn't around to watch teany during its gestation period.

I would talk to Kelly every few days and she would tell me about the progress that she was making and how she was trying to negotiate with contractors and plumbers and city officials and so on and so on, and I felt bad that she was dealing with all of this on her own, but it was hard to be of too much assistance when, a) I was on an airplane every day, and b) I knew nothing about trying to open a restaurant.

It was also around this time that I went to Japan. I like Japan, don't get me wrong, but sitting in a Japanese hotel room for ten hours a day for four days doing interviews while incredibly jet-lagged is not the nicest way to spend one's time. Did you see *Lost in Translation*? See, that was glamorous. They sang karaoke, they danced, they drank. Me, I just sat in a hotel room doing interviews with translators for ten hours a day. I did get to go to this great restaurant called Café 8, but apart from that I was exhausted and unhappy.

When I was in Amsterdam, I had been doing twelve hours of promo/interviews a day with no days off, and Kelly and I were talking on the phone, and we decided that we should break up. I was looking at a promotional and concert tour that was scheduled to last eighteen months, and we both thought that we would be better off as friends and business partners. At least I had this great chocolate soy milk to kind of heal the pain. And alcohol. But that doesn't always help, now does it?

My crazy traveling was winding down a bit, and toward the end of April, I was even allowed to come home for a while! So I came home and stopped at teany en route from the airport to my apartment and, lo and behold, teany was real! I couldn't believe it. Poor Kelly had lost twenty pounds, and she looked like a weary little squirrel, but we had a teany. Or at least I thought we had a teany. From Kelly's perspective we didn't have all sorts of things that one would need to open a restaurant, but from my perspective it looked amazing and my heart swelled with pride.

I had to go away again, and once more found myself saying good-bye to Kelly (once my girlfriend, now my friend and business partner) and leaving her to try to put the finishing touches on teany. I do have to say that if you're ever thinking of opening a restaurant and you have a partner and you're thinking about how to divide the labor, I strongly suggest that you get your partner to do all of the hard work. It really will make your life a lot easier. It might make your partner insane and resentful, but, in the end, they'll thank you for the fantastic experience. Or so I imagine. I'm being facetious by the way. Well, I'm being

facetious about the "get your partner to do the hard work" suggestion. I'm not being facetious when I say that it might make your partner insane. So after being away for a few more weeks I returned home in May for . . .

Opening night! Kelly and I were both losing our minds. I was losing my mind because I was releasing a record and traveling around the world and doing interviews and planning tours and making videos and I didn't have even five free minutes in a day, and Kelly was losing her mind because she was running around trying to figure out how to have an opening night party in a restaurant that wasn't ready for an opening night party.

But there we were, opening night of little teany. A Sunday, if I remember correctly, and it rained. But everyone showed up. All of my friends, all of Kelly's friends, the neighbors, the police, even Matt Groening hung out for a while drawing pictures for the well-wishers.

Now please keep in mind that teany is very small (thus *teany*) and it's crowded when there are thirty people sitting inside. At our party we had around two hundred to three hundred people. It was very chaotic, and very stressful (more so for Kelly, obviously, who was trying to keep everyone fed and happy), but it was also very exciting. We had taken a hungover idea (that being an idea born of a hangover) and turned it into a real reality. And teany, thanks to Kelly's remarkable efforts, looked wonderful, and the food was great and the drinks were tasty and I was proud and happy and Kelly was proud and exhausted.

a history of the lower east side (and our ancestors)

1895 Eastern European Immigration

Fact: In the late nineteenth century, the Lower East Side was the most densely populated place on the planet. It was a new home for hundreds of thousands of immigrants, all living on top of each other and packed into the Lower East Side of Manhattan. If you had walked through the Lower East Side around this time, you would have found rows of tenement houses, Gothic Revival, Romanesque, and Moorish-style synagogues, Catholic churches, bath houses, and banks, as well as a progressive library and an institute designed specifically to help immigrants ease into American life. There was even a Yiddish vaudeville theater and boxing venue where our local movie theater now resides!

Fiction: Here we have our ancestors who came to America full of hope but also full of trepidation and worry. Yetzl Teekne and his long-suffering wife, Gelda, left their cucumber farm in Belarus to come and seek a better life in the New World.

1919
PROHIBITION

Fiction: Unfortunately, Yetzl Teekne quickly turned to drink after fathering fourteen children with Gelda and some of the local "women of easy virtue."

"Where is your pay packet you ne'er-do-well!?" Gelda would cry.

"Ach, leave me in peace, woman, and fetch me a bucket of beer!"

"All day I scrub the floors and mind the young'ns, and you play jackanapes with your hooligan associates!"

"I shall drown my sorrows with another bucket of beer, woman!"

Fact: The stories that come from the Lower East Side during the Prohibition era are legendary. Beginning in 1919, Prohibition set the stage for standoffs between politicians and gangsters, with the governor of New York, Al Smith (who was born on the Lower East Side), strongly opposing Prohibition, and infamous gang leader Bugsy Siegel controlling the Lower East Side by hijacking mafiosi shipments of booze destined for his territory. However, going through Bugsy wasn't the only way one could get their hands on the illegal substance called alcohol, and many men quietly (making sure Bugsy didn't find out) concocted their very own home brews.

1944 World War II

Fiction: Two of Yetzl and Gelda's children are pictured here after V-E Day. Pictured on the right are Doris Teekne and her brother Glenn Teekne. Glenn is shown delivering Doris to her husband, Franklin Little (off camera), in a time-honored Belarussian tradition. Oh you kid…!

Fact: "Send a salami to your boy in the army!" advertised Katz's, the most famous kosher deli on the Lower East Side, during wartime. Despite the war, the Lower East Side continued to be a bustling marketplace filled with peddlers and hagglers. Because most of the shop owners were Jewish, the shops were closed on Saturday in observance of the Sabbath, but open on Sundays, violating New York's blue laws against operating business on the Christian Sabbath, making the Lower East Side *the* place for bargain hunters to shop on Sundays.

Among the street markets, tenements, synagogues, and churches, you would have come across victory gardens had you visited the Lower East Side in the early 1940s. Facing widespread food rationing, these were gardens that were created in the spirit of self-reliance so that industrially grown food could be released for the troops abroad. These innovative gardens were abandoned at the end of the war when rationing became unnecessary and frozen food became popular.

tea needs the lamb bleating sky machine
— Anonymous (but aren't we all, man?)

Wrap your soul in dollars, Business Leech,
You can eat your dollars, but do they eat you?
I hold your horn, and the wind blows
And all the little cats know
And the tea grows . . .

Outside the man is wailing, lament young,
Saxophones and banana slides to the suburbs
Big land outside the monkey planes
But Charlie Chaplin knows
And the tea grows . . .

Snap away to the Finland station
Glide back and see the mist of strawberry believing
The man will keep his feet down on the grass . . .
But the fly crows
And the tea grows . . .

1954
THE BEAT GENERATION

Fiction: Pictured here are Yetzl and Gelda's two youngest children, Jean-Luc and Simone Teekne. Rejecting bourgeoisie society and its phony values, Jean-Luc and Simone chose to live as bohemians in the very same cold-water flat in which they had grown up. They ran an earlier incarnation of teany that they called The Outside Morning Glory Antonin Artaud Tea Hovel. Oftentimes, Yetzel and Gelda would gather with their friends and recite poetry to the ubiquitous and hypnotic beat of the humble bongo drum. We recently found one of their poems and we wanted to reprint it here for your general edification.

Fact: At the start of the cold war, the Lower East Side served as a back-drop for marginalized artists and poets, who gathered in the cramped, sub-standard tenement housing for readings, art shows, and conferences about how their ranks could have an impact on making the world more open to their "vision." Self-published books of poetry, mimeographed in the same basements that these forward-thinking people met in, were passed on to independent bookstores across the country, forming artistic alliances from coast to coast.

iced tea

Fact: By the late 1960s and early 1970s, the Lower East Side, along with the rest of New York, was quickly becoming a city of abandoned plots from the Victory Garden era, crumbled storefronts, arsoned buildings, and vacant lots being used mainly by drug dealers, prostitutes, and thieves who needed somewhere to store their stolen goods. Due to a citywide fiscal crisis, the city's government wasn't doing much to clean up the district, so a group of people calling themselves the Green Guerrillas decided that they were going to clean it up.

In a (very) civil form of disobedience, the Green Guerrillas began to take over abandoned lots on the Lower East Side and turn them into parks. Their first garden was on the corner of Houston and Bowery, and, eventually, they created over seventy parks on the Lower East Side and inspired countless groups to do the same in their own neighborhoods. Even though what they were doing was technically illegal, by the mid-1970s, the Green Guerrillas had won over many government officials who helped push through statewide and national programs for community gardens and parks development. Still in existence, the Green Guerillas are directly responsible for more than 850 gardens and green areas.

1970 ☮
The Counterculture

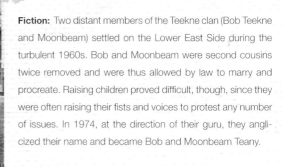

Fiction: Two distant members of the Teekne clan (Bob Teekne and Moonbeam) settled on the Lower East Side during the turbulent 1960s. Bob and Moonbeam were second cousins twice removed and were thus allowed by law to marry and procreate. Raising children proved difficult, though, since they were often raising their fists and voices to protest any number of issues. In 1974, at the direction of their guru, they anglicized their name and became Bob and Moonbeam Teany.

PUNK ROCK! 1980

Fiction: Bob and Moonbeam, possibly as a result of unintentional genetic manipulation and/or inbreeding, ended up giving birth to two sets of identical twins, Alexxxandra and Shazeeel (the girls) and Robo and D-Nice (the boys). Alexxxandra and Robo were caught up in the burgeoning culture of punk rock.

Fact:

Punk

in New York was already well established on the Lower East Side by the late 1970s, with bands like Blondie, the Ramones, Television, Talking Heads, and the Patti Smith Group, living and performing in what was then a very dingy, run-down part of town. By 1980, this scene was beginning to branch out into an influential subculture, morphing the world of art and music with the help of visionaries such as Jean-Michel Basquiat and Keith Haring. The impact of these young artists was apparent even in the neighborhoods they lived in; they used the streets and walls of the city as one enormous canvas, and you could find their now legendary work in many corners, crevices, old buildings, fresh cement—wherever they could create. Nowhere better represented the cross-cultural energy that was surging through the Lower East Side than ABC NO Rio, an activists' and artists' space that opened in 1980.

Reminiscent of a YMCA, ABC NO Rio began as a community-minded art center, which had among other things a print shop, a zine (underground publications) library, and a darkroom, and allowed everything from poetry readings to hardcore music concerts, where bands like the Cro-Mags held their all-ages Saturday afternoon shows.

Birth of
HIP HOP

1980

Fact: Though hip-hop was born in the Bronx, the young Caribbean and Latin American people who had immigrated to the Lower East Side were quick to adopt it as part of their culture as well. These recent immigrants contributed greatly to the Lower East Side's art scene, and the street murals, drawings, paintings, scribbles, and tags that the Lower East Side artists were so fond of creating were not unlike the graffiti murals and train pieces by artists in the hip-hop community of the Bronx. It was all art, and all for the public (as opposed to the galleries). Because these two subcultures shared this vision, their worlds were destined to meet and create a new kind of urban culture. By the mideighties, these progressive groups at the opposite ends of Manhattan island had closed the gap between music and art, and neither would ever be same again.

Fiction: The other Teany twins, Shazeeel and D-Nice, were heavily involved in the burgeoning world of hip-hop and break dancing. Unfortunately Shazeeel and D-Nice were not actually any good at break dancing, so they instead have devoted their lives to helping their adopted children, Kelly and Moby (any resemblance is bizarre and coincidental), with their plans for world domination.

teany today

2

Chapter 2: Afternoon Tea for Swingers

We at teany think that afternoon tea is above all, fun. You can eat everything with your hands. And there are so many different flavors. It's like when you go to a party and there are tons of fantastic hors d'oeuvres and you want to eat them all, but you (like our duchess friend) don't want to be seen as a glutton, so you only eat a few. Afternoon tea is nothing but tasty little morsels of goodness, all for you, and for whomever you want to have your afternoon tea with. And just so you know, it's not a sin to have your afternoon tea at other times of the day besides the afternoon. Have it for breakfast! Have it at midnight! We're not here to tell you how to live your life, just how to make the most fun out of eating.

Afternoon tea usually consists of four main components: tea, tea sandwiches, scones, and petit fours. Tea—any kind of tea will do. Yes, Darjeeling, English breakfast, or Earl Grey are the most commonly served at afternoon tea, but a nice Japanese green or fruity herbal goes just as well.

Tea sandwiches are simple sandwiches (two fillings usually) made with the crusts cut off, and cut into quarters. Traditionally, a cucumber and butter sandwich is served, or sweet little shrimps (happy!) made into a salad (sad). But you can make a tea sandwich with any tasty filling. Peanut butter and mushrooms! Marmite and pickle! (We aren't actually suggesting those; we just want you to feel free to be creative with your tea sandwiches.) Why don't you start off by trying out the recipes we have conveniently laid out in this chapter.

artichoke and garlic spread with mixed greens sandwich

Filling

1½ tablespoons crushed garlic

1 can (15–16 ounces) artichoke hearts

1 tablespoon veganaise or nayonaise

1 teaspoon mustard

1 tablespoon sugar

1 tablespoon red wine vinegar

   salt to taste

1 tablespoon extra virgin olive oil

Sandwich

8 slices white bread

Mixed greens to taste

Blend all filling ingredients except the olive oil in a food processor. Drizzle the olive oil through as it spins around. And voila! Gourmet tea sandwich spread accomplished!

Spread the artichoke mixture on both slices of bread for each tea sandwich you make, and heartily fill with mixed greens, or one particular green of your choice, if you have a favorite. Close the sandwich, cut the crusts off, and cut into fourths.

Makes 16 tea sandwich pieces

Some Other Tea Sandwich Ideas

Cucumber and Basil: As simple as this sandwich seems, the taste is surprisingly flavorful and refreshing. Just spread margarine on both slices of bread before you fill the sandwich with thin cucumber slices and fresh basil. This one might end up being your favorite.

Tofu Cream Cheese: If you can get your hands on some tofu cream cheese, you can mix some herbs into it (such as dill, sage, thyme, oregano, etc.) and make a sandwich out of the spread and another, crunchier filling such as alfalfa sprouts.

Olive Tapenade: You can also take the Olive Tapenade (see page 66) and mix 1 part tapenade to 3 parts tofu cream cheese. This

½ tablespoon corn syrup

6 phylo dough cups

1 teaspoon freshly grated lime rind

Blend tofu and lime juice. Thoroughly blend mixture with pudding mix. Add the soy cream cheese and corn syrup, and mix until smooth.

Fill phylo dough cups (found in freezer section) with key lime mix. Sprinkle the precious little key lime pies with the grated lime rind, and store in the fridge (in the back, where no one can see, including yourself, since they are just *begging* to be sampled) until ready to serve.

Makes 6 petit fours

Simple Chocolatey Chocolate Cake

¾ cup white flour

⅓ cup cocoa

¼ teaspoon baking soda

¼ teaspoon salt

½ cup sugar

¼ cup vegetable oil

½ cup cold water

1 teaspoon vanilla extract

1 tablespoon vinegar

1 personal-sized bar of vegan chocolate (it can have nuts or fruit in it if you want)

Mix all ingredients, except the vegan chocolate bar, together by hand until mixture is smooth. Batter will look liquidy, it's okay. Pour mixture into round 8-inch cake pan. Break the vegan chocolate bar into chip-sized pieces and sprinkle on top of the cake batter (these pieces will sink into the cake). Bake at 375° F. for 20 to 30 minutes. (Stick a toothpick in after 20 minutes, and do so every 2 minutes until the cake is done, when the toothpick comes out clean.) Let cool, then cut into pieces (the shape and size is up to you. I suggest bite-sized) and decorate with whatever you love to eat chocolate with!

Makes 12 petit fours

Lulu's Tea Party!

This is Lulu.

We may be biased (as she and her mom are teany regulars),
but we think that she is the cutest little girl in the entire world.

This is Lulu, her friend, and their stuffed animals having a tea party. Notice Lulu's forthright eye contact with the camera. We think that Lulu might be the first female president of the United States. We would vote for her.

This is the "food and hats" picture. Notice the tasty food and the festive hats. And the absurdly cute little tea set. Kids rule.

Yes, this is a cute picture. We're well aware of that fact. That's why we included it. If only every day involved a cute tea party with stuffed animals sitting on newspapers.

This is Lulu pretending that she is the singer in an eighties heavy metal band. Dokken, possibly, or Poison. It was always hard for us to tell them apart, to be honest with you.

Pictured here are Lulu and her friend discussing the pernicious lack of transparency in the operations of the International Monetary Fund.

It is a rule in teany that every tea party has to involve 5 minutes of dancing. Here Lulu is dancing to "Anarchy in the UK" by the Sex Pistols.

Every now and then you have to interrupt your tea party and play monster.

a few interesting historical tidbits

When Moby and I opened teany, we wanted a simple little tea shop where everyone could find something that they would like to eat and drink, where people could meet other interesting people, where the neighborhood artists and late-day risers could stroll in at 4:00 P.M. for breakfast, and where everyone could feel at home. As far as atmosphere was concerned, there wasn't any place in our neighborhood that felt the way we wanted our teahouse to feel. So, being naïve and pompous, we thought that we were creating something new.

Oh were we wrong! It turns out that all the attributes that we wanted our teahouse to have, hundreds of other teahouses in New York City had—about eighty years ago. Really! I couldn't believe it either! But it's true. It all started in a little neighborhood called Greenwich Village.

The low rent and quaint attractiveness of Greenwich Village are what originally attracted artists, professional women, gays, socialists, anarchists, expatriates and radicals to the area in the early 1900s. These were modern thinkers living unconventional lives at a time when being unconventional was considered undesirable at best and dangerous at worst. Professional, independent women (when I say professional I mean as in having a job, not to be confused with "the oldest profession," if you know what I mean) didn't have it easy. Women weren't even allowed into bars or restaurants if not accompanied by a male, never mind being considered competent enough to support themselves in any real way. And gays? In the beginning of the twenty-first century, there are still some places in this world where a gay person will be abused for being "out." Can you imagine what it was like a hundred years ago? Anarchists, socialists, and ex-pats didn't have it so easy either, considering that the red scare got more than a few forward-thinking, good-intentioned, politically active people deported or locked up.

This was a smart, but persecuted bunch. Or, they weren't exactly persecuted, but would have been (and I'm sure some were) had they not chosen to live in Greenwich Village. And you would think that all of these people living together with all their unconventional lifestyles would have created chaos in the neighborhood, but oddly enough, it created a bunch of teahouses instead.

about teahouses in new york city

All these people needed places to hang out and be their "radical" and "socially rebellious" selves. Or really, just to eat, chat, and exchange ideas. So naturally, they decided to create a bunch of radical teahouses for their new, modern, bohemian lifestyles. Most important, these teahouses needed to keep the same hours they did so most of them were open all night and sometimes during the day—but never before 4:00 P.M. Considering the hours that these people and places kept, I'm sure that not all of their tea was served to them steaming (considering that Prohibition was beginning to take hold, people had to find creative ways of getting wasted).

By 1917, there were so many teahouses that *The New York Times* called Greenwich Village a place "whose inhabitants make their living by keeping restaurants for each other." To give you an example of the density of teahouses in this area, in one remarkable four-story Greenwich Village building, there were no less than six teahouses (according to a diligent teahouse researcher named Jan Whitaker). However, all of those teahouses couldn't fit into actual business or apartment spaces (or maybe it was just too conventional for this radical bunch) so stables, workshop spaces, attics, roofs, and basements were transformed into intimate teahouses through the clever use of candles, exposed brick, flowers, and brightly colored paints. And most tearooms were small, able to seat only around twenty people at a time.

Doesn't sound so bad, right? Sounds a little bit like teany, except that we're open during the day and get all kinds of nice people here, not just crazy radicals. And maybe we were a little disappointed to find out that we are far from the first to think of the idea of an all-welcoming, casual teahouse, but after learning about the tradition of teahouses in New York, we're genuinely proud that teany is part of it all, not too sound too sappy . . .

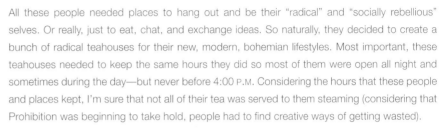

3

Chapter 3: Health and/or Beauty

We don't claim to be experts or anything, but being that both Moby and I are completely paranoid about chemicals, we have been relatively successful in finding ways around some conventional drugstore-type products for our health and beauty needs. All recipes and suggestions in this chapter are really simple and inexpensive—no making salves or elixirs or tonics or tinctures, or anything like that. So just say What the heck one day and try a few out.

dr. moby's health tips . . .

mouthwash

Is anyone else freaked out by the fact that you're not supposed to swallow mouthwash? If it's good enough to put in your mouth, it shouldn't be so bad in the rest of your body. If you happen to swallow some of this concoction, you won't have to go to the emergency room. The goldenrod and elder flower both have strong astringent properties, the licorice root will create a sweet numbness in the back of the throat, and the peppermint refreshes.

6 cups water

½ tablespoon loose goldenrod

½ tablespoon loose elder flower

½ tablespoon loose licorice root

1 tablespoon loose peppermint

Heat the water until it is almost boiling, and add the goldenrod, elder flower, licorice root, and peppermint. Bring the pot temperature down to medium, and let the teas simmer loosely (with cover on pot) for 10 minutes. Turn off the heat, and let the mixture cool with the cover on the pot. Once it has reached room temperature, pour the mouthwash in a plastic or glass bottle and store in the fridge. Use it at least twice a day after brushing, but be sure to put it back in the fridge when not in use! This stuff will last one glorious week!

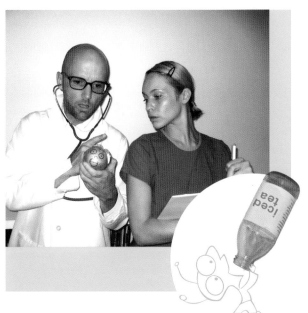

dr. moby's cure for
caffeine addiction

Okay, we've established that tea is good for you. It has antioxidants and polyphenols and vitamins and minerals and all sorts of things that will keep the Grim Reaper away from you and busy with the non-green-tea-drinking people on the planet. But tea also has caffeine. And caffeine, in small quantities, is not such a bad thing. Personally I love the caffeine, but too much caffeine makes me feel like a crystal-meth addict at the end of a particularly rough bender.

Now suppose you don't want your tea to be caffeinated? What can you do? Well, let Dr. Moby (not a real doctor) try to help. You could buy tea that has already been decaffeinated. That's an option, but it kind of limits the teas that are available for your consumption. Better yet, you can decaffeinate your own tea.

"But won't I need fancy equipment and tea robots and whatnot in order to decaffeinate my tea?" I can hear you saying. No. One secret to the world of tea is that decaffeinating it is one of the easiest things you'll ever do. See, caffeine is the most volatile compound in tea, and it's pretty much all released in the first 30 seconds after the tea leaves come into contact with hot water. So here's what you do if you want decaffeinated tea:

- Make tea as you normally would.
- Let it steep for 45 seconds.
- Dump out the liquid.
- Add hot water again, and steep the tea as you normally would.

Now what you're left with in your second pot/cup of tea is decaffeinated tea. Easy. Cheap. Fun. Decaffeinated.

clotting agent

Sounds technical, but it's really simple: If you cut yourself shaving, or overzealously pick a zit, you don't want to be bleeding and red all day from it. So get some horsetail! Not real horsetail, of course, the herb called horsetail. Horsetail helps support regeneration of the connective tissue because of its high silica and calcium contents. If you apply some aloe right after the horsetail, it will leave your skin in the best condition nature could ever recommend in order to repair itself.

You can get horsetail at an herb store, the tea section of any good health food store (just cut open the tea bags and voila! Dried horsetail), or online (Alvita brand is pretty easy to find). You could also grow it, but if you put it in your garden, it will take over and kill everything. This grass is a survivor. In fact, it's prehistoric—dinosaurs snacked on it. So grow the dinosaur snack/clotting agent in a pot instead.

To make this wonderful healing liquid, boil 1½ pints of water and 1 ounce of fresh horsetail or ¾ ounce of dried horsetail. Let it simmer until the mixture boils down to 1 pint. Allow it to cool and apply the liquid to your cut or zit with a cotton ball. Keep applying until the bleeding stops, which will be soon, I promise.

lovely kelly's beauty tip . . .

puffy eye tea treatment

Whether due to too much to drink the night before, a little too much crying at a sappy movie, or even too much staring at the computer, nothing relieves puffy eyes better than old tea bags that have been refrigerated. By old, I mean a day or two. Not a week. That's gross.

Black, oolong, and green tea bags work best for this, and I wouldn't use fruity herbals unless you want big magenta circles dyed onto your face for a day. Steep two tea bags (black, oolong, green, or white tea) and squeeze out the excess liquid. Refrigerate them for at least an hour and then place over eyes for at least 5 minutes. This should noticeably take away the puffiness.

HINT: Want to appear sick at work? (So you can go home early and watch that Johnny Depp marathon on TBS—it's okay, we've all done it. They start out with *Benny and Joon* and end it with *Cry Baby*. How do they expect us to resist?) Here's what you do: Put fruity herbal tea bags on your eyes, tell them you think you have pinkeye, and they'll send you home immediately. (That was a joke. Please don't actually do that. Or if you do, don't tell anyone that you got the pinkeye tip from this book, please.

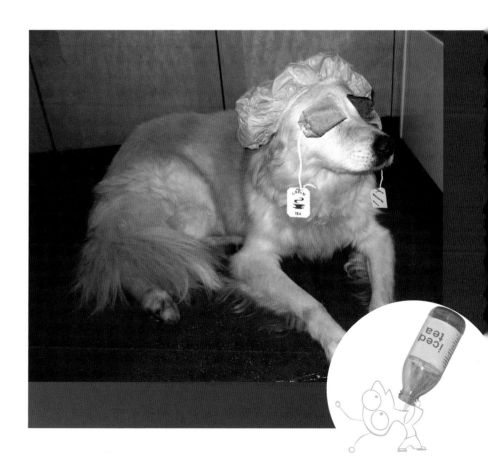

dr. moby's . . . hangover cure

Okay, the truth be told, I'm currently enjoying a period of extended sobriety. Or is it extended period of sobriety? You get the point. But I'm well acquainted with terrible brain-melting, body-destroying hangovers, and I'm here to share with you my personal cure for making hangovers either a) go away or b) not be so bad. (Although it should be said that the best cure for a hangover is to avoid excessive drinking in the first place. I just felt the need to be responsible and say that. Sorry.)

The operative word in my hangover prescription is rehydrating. Or rehydration. Drinking a lot of liquid will rehydrate your body and will help to flush the toxins out of your system. Before going to bed the night of your alcoholic bender, drink a lot of water. In fact, try to drink a lot of water while you're drinking alcohol. Or, rather, in between your alcoholic drinks. One alcoholic drink followed by one glass of water is a good rule if you can manage it. So drink a lot of water. And before going to bed, take two aspirin or ibuprofen.

Once you're awake and ambulatory, drink some more water. And juice. And tea. And more water. And more juice. And more tea. What tea should you drink? I would suggest a nice green tea because you are going to be drinking

a lot of tea if you use my suggestions, and you don't want all the caffeine of a black tea. But if you don't want any caffeine on your hungover day, you may as well not even get out of bed.

Eating salty, rich, yet healthy food is the other component to overcoming even your worst hangover. Don't go crazy, but have some fun and try to have a breakfast that is kind of salty/savory and healthy but rich. At teany, for example, a great hangover breakfast is our everything bagel with olive–tofu cream cheese and cucumber and tomato slices accompanied by a big ol' pot of gunpowder green tea (that's just a little bit oversteeped because bitter tea is nice when you're hungover) and a lot of water and orange juice. However, since you probably won't be getting up until the afternoon, why not skip the breakfast food and dive directly into lunch. This will allow you to try the best hangover food around: the Cashew Butter Sandwich.

teany comic
by moby

teany started with a hangover.

See, three years ago Kelly and I had BAD hangovers.

So we opened a cafe that served very nice hangover food.

We called it teany. Why teany?

1. teany (teenie) cos we're little.

2. teany cos we have 97 teas.

3. teany cos we're in new york.

And now we have teany in a bottle.

Peach Berry Green Tea is my favorite.

Kelly's favorite is Vanilla Berry l libiscus.

Thank you!

Oh, teany is at 90 Rivington.
Come visit!

lovely kelly's . . .

facial steam

Does your skin ever do that thing where it makes your pores look like craters? Yeah, mine too. It totally stinks. But let's face it, sometimes facial pores do have to work extra hard to get out all those impurities. So why not help them out with this gentle facial steam? I'm telling you, a five-minute steam using these herbs (that are also nice as teas!) twice a week will leave your skin gleaming and seemingly pore-less. It feels *so* good too, and smells amazing.

What you will need to get seemingly pore-less perfection:

1 gallon water

2 tablespoons loose linden flowers for antiseptic and antibiotic effects (also has calming properties to help reduce stress and anxiety)

2 tablespoons loose, dried blue violet leaves and/or flowers for antiseptic properties and glorious scent

2 tablespoons loose lemongrass for antiseptic properties and astringent effect (binds the skin to make pores appear smaller!). Lemongrass also has traces of essential oils for all of those aroma therapy fans out there.

Bring water to a boil, and turn the heat down to low. Add all the herbs to the water and let simmer for 10 minutes with the cover on. Take the pot off the flame, and set it on a low table or the floor. You need to be able to sit comfortably with your face at least 8 inches from the surface of the water. Take the cover off the pot and drape a towel over your head and the pot to trap in the steam. Move your face farther away from the surface of the water if the steam feels too hot. Breathe in, breathe out. Breathe in, breathe out.

Ahhhhh.

dr. moby's *(not a real doctor)* saying for the day:

"nature is our medicine cabinet"

Okay, don't actually *say* that, because if you say that you might get looks of derision or threats of violence from your friends. And for good reason because it is a pretty lame thing to say, even if it's true.

So, being that nature is our medicine cabinet, let's talk about herbs that alleviate anxiety. See, just as nature gives us an abundance of legal and illegal stimulants and psychotropics, nature also gives us an abundance of legal and illegal sedatives, some of which I'm going to talk about here.

My favorites of the legal sedatives are kava kava, chamomile, and valerian. Chamomile is the most gentle of the sedatives. (In fact, truth be told, it might not really have any great sedative qualities, but it looks and tastes nice; and it seems to be relaxing, so don't rain on my parade, okay?) And valerian is the most extreme. Rumor has it that Valium was invented as a synthetic version of valerian. And I'm sure that Valium is a nice relaxant, but I think that I'll stick with valerian, what with its being herbal and all. When I've traveled and had jet lag, valerian has proven to be a remarkable soporific. And valerian taken with kava kava can have pretty remarkable sedative and antianxiety properties. But as your doctor *(again, not a real doctor)*, I can't say that you should go around mixing your own amalgams of herbal sedatives. Leave it to the professionals, and there are lots of professionals.

Any trip to a health food store will yield a plethora of herbal antianxiety/soporific/calming pills, teas, tinctures, etc.; and most of them are quite good. Don't abuse them, and if you're on other medication, you should check with your doctor before taking anything. But if you're jet-lagged and not on other medication; well, have a cup of valerian tea, and it should really do the trick and help you fall asleep and stay asleep.

chamomile and lemongrass hair rinse

Do you ever take a shower and don't want to wash your hair (because you don't want it to be "fluffy"), so you just rinse it but feel like you should be putting something in it? This is the stuff to put in it.

6 cups water
2 tablespoons loose chamomile tea
2 tablespoons loose lemongrass tea

Bring the water to a boil in a medium-sized pot and then turn the burner to the lowest setting. Add the chamomile and lemongrass teas and let simmer for 10 minutes with the cover on. Take the pot off the burner and let sit (with the cover still on) until the mixture is cool. Strain the tea so that it's just liquid. Put the liquid in a spray bottle (Use a funnel! Don't make a mess!), refrigerate, and take out only when ready to use in the shower.

When using the rinse in the shower, spray your hair with it toward the end, only partially rinsing it out, or simply wringing it out. Use again after hair is towel dried for more weight and fragrance without greasiness. The chamomile will undoubtedly make your hair shiny while the traces of essential oils in the lemongrass will coat and protect the hair.

HINT: If you want to add more weight, thickness, and fragrance to your rinse (and hence, your hair), add a few drops of essential oil. You can even get inexpensive nonessential oil such as the ones that The Body Shop carries. The Egyptian musk oil is an especially delightful, even sexy, fragrance you can add.

dr. moby's . . . cure for the common cold

Okay, it's January, and everyone around you is dying of a cold or some flu-related illness. What can you do to protect yourself (apart from some sort of DNA manipulation that will turn you into a superhuman who is impervious to cold germs)? You can take Dr. Moby's Cure for the Common Cold:

1 thumb-sized piece of ginger, chopped into little bits
2 cloves garlic, chopped into little bits
½ teaspoon cayenne powder

Take all of these ingredients and put them in the bottom of a mug. Then pour boiling water over the ingredients (careful, boiling water's hot. I'm a master of the obvious). And let steep for 5 to 10 minutes. After 5 to 10 minutes, strain the liquid into a separate mug and drink it. Drink slowly, because it is pretty harsh and disgusting. It's akin to drinking battery acid, but I really have found that it does great things to/for your immune defenses. See, I care. Even if it does seem sadistic on my part that I'm asking you to drink something so disgusting. It really is good for you.

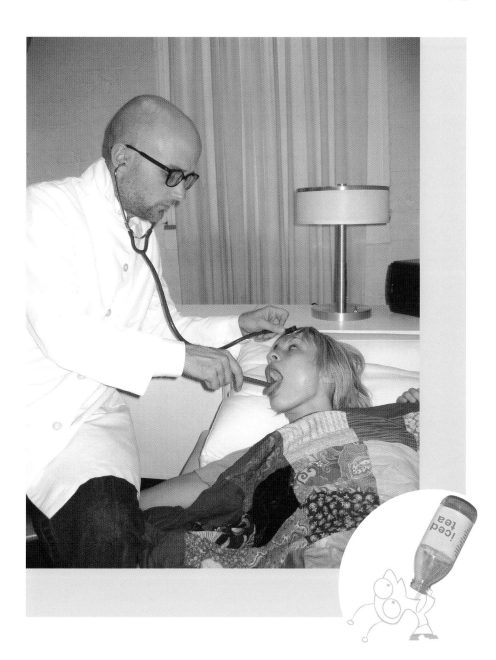

dr. moby's . . .

compress for minor cuts, skin irritations, swelling, bruises, and burns*

This compress is especially nice to have around if you have very sensitive skin that tends to react to everything that you put on it, or if you have accident-prone children and you don't want to always be smearing them with chemicals. Also, this compress should be made ahead of time and kept in the fridge (will keep for a week or so) because it's best if used cold to prevent further swelling.

What you will need for your chemical-free, all-healing compress:

1 gallon water

2 tablespoons red clover, for its antibiotic, anti-inflamatory, antiviral, antifungal, and antimicrobial properties

2 tablespoons goldenseal root, for its antiseptic, antibiotic, and clotting properties

2 tablespoons comfrey root, to soothe wounds and stimulate new cell growth

1 tablespoon elder flower, for its anti-inflammatory and anticatarrhal (mucus secretion) properties

Bring the water to a boil. Add all herbs, turn to low, and let simmer with a cover on for 20 minutes. Strain the liquid, and refrigerate. When ready to use, dip a facecloth into the liquid and partially wring it out, keeping a generous amount of the liquid in the cloth. Treat until wound is clotted or until inflammation or irritations have gone down.

*Obviously, we stress the term minor here. This compress is not going to heal a broken arm or make gangrene go away.

BOO BOO!

lovely kelly's
rooibos dry skin facial

ooibos has alpha hydroxy properties, which means it acts as a mild acid that dissolves dry skin, providing exfoliation without having to scrub. To get noticeable relief from dry patches, apply rooibos tea bags directly onto the dry spots such as your face, elbows, or even heels. Depending on how the dry the skin you are treating is, you should see results in 3 to 7 days.

Get enough rooibos tea bags (or make your own from loose tea and empty tea bags) to cover the surface on your skin that you are treating. (It takes about 5 bags to cover half of your face, and then the teas can be immediately resteeped and applied to the areas that weren't treated before.) Soak the tea bags in boiling water for just 2 minutes. Take the tea bags out of the water and put them into bowls. Don't discard that water, drink it! Put the bags in the freezer for 3 minutes, or until cool enough to put on your skin. The tea bags should still be warm, even steaming, when they are applied to the area being treated. Place the bags directly on dry spots and let them sit there until completely cool. If you put rooibos tea bags all over your face, it makes for an intense facial by opening the pores for a steam clean as well as gently and effectively exfoliating.

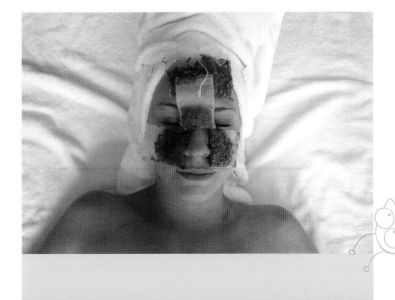

dr. moby's . . .
ginkgo tip

As your doctor (NOTE: *Moby's not a real doctor*), I feel it is incumbent upon me to talk about ginkgo biloba. Ginkgo biloba (okay, let's just call it ginkgo for short, okay?) is one of my favorite herbalmedicinals (and yes, I did just invent that Germanically long word).

Before I delve into ginkgo and its remarkable properties, let me first tell you a little bit about the history of ginkgo. Okay, for starters, ginkgo is a plant that dates back to the time of dinosaurs, and it has remained virtually unchanged for hundreds of millions of years. Yes, it's true, and as your doctor (NOTE: *not a real doctor*), I thought that you'd like to know. Ginkgo is old. Ancient. From the bygone mists of prehistory itself, when humans were just furry little nothings that ate seeds in the crevices of some dirty old caves and tried not get eaten. (Thus: Anxiety. But that's a different story.)

Ginkgo, apart from having antioxidant properties, does some very interesting things to the circulatory system, especially the circulatory system in the mother of all organs: the brain. See, ginkgo facilitates blood flow in the circulatory system, which just happens to be where blood flows. (I'm so smart.) And speaking from subjective experience, it can actually increase cognitive functioning. I'm not saying that it will boost your I.Q., but it can make you a little bit sharper up in the brain department.

And as a little factual aside: Did you know that the rare and ancient ginkgo biloba tree is not actually as rare as you might think? It is, in fact, one of the most common trees growing in New York City. The reason for its Big Apple ubiquity is that it's such a tough little tree that it doesn't succumb to the rigors of city life. And it has a canopy that grows above the trucks, so it doesn't get in the way of the nice people who bring us teany-brand bottled beverages.

And, my final little bit of trivia, you can eat ginkgo nuts. Yes, in fact many Chinese restaurants use them as special ingredients in Chinese cooking. And if you live in or near Chinatown (as Kelly and I both do) you can see little old Chinese ladies picking ginkgo nuts in the East River Park in the morning when they're done doing their tai chi. It's true. But as with all things, go easy on the ginkgo if you decide to try it.

lovely kelly's . . .
tea bath

Put tea in the bath! Black, oolong, green, and white teas as well as flowery herbals are all soothing on the skin and won't dry your skin like traditional, overly perfumed bath and bubble products. In fact, you could take a tea bath every day and not worry about its drying your skin or leaving you covered in a weird film. Chamomile and linden are especially nice, since they have calming properties. Lavender, mint, and rosebuds are wonderful too! Stay away from pu-erhs (twice-fermented tea), herbal fruit teas, and herbal root teas. Putting any of those in the tub would just be weird and dirty and sticky. Also, before draining the bath water, put a filter of some kind (like a coffee filter) over the drain so your calming tea bath doesn't become a plumbing nightmare. To prepare your bath, just sprinkle some loose tea (about 1/4 ounce) in your luxuriously warm bath water.

4

Chapter 4: Caffeine Is Your Friend

If you open a teahouse you have to love (or at least appreciate)
caffeine. Not all of the drinks sold at teany are caffeinated, but most
of them are. Here we have "bios" of some of our more interesting
caffeinated teas.

ilver needle

This tea is sorta like the champagne of all teas in that it's rare, expensive, and an acquired taste. It's rare and expensive because it's only grown in one place (in the high mountains of the Fujian province in China) and is harvested only once a year (in early spring). And as if that's not rare enough, the leaves also need to be plucked within forty-eight hours of the first buds' becoming fully mature. And there are definitely people there (in the Fujian province) who make sure that everyone prepares this tea according to its strict requirements, which include a rapid firing and drying of the tea leaves in order to keep them in their pure and natural state.

And why is it an acquired taste? Because it takes patience and a delicate palate to be able to fully appreciate the silver needle. This tea takes any-where from 10 to 15 minutes to steep, and even when fully steeped, it doesn't have much body. Its cup color is nothing to write home about either. Some people call it light and airy while others call it a scam. And still others say, "Well, if it's good enough for royalty, then it's good enough for me." You see, the silver needle has a reputation for being one of China's most famous and sought-after teas, and, in ancient times, this tea was used as a tribute tea for royalty and dignitaries.

But that's not why you should drink this tea. You should drink it (or at least try it) because it is a white tea, and all white teas have more polyphenols than green tea, and polyphenols prevent cancer, basically. Also, this tea has very little caffeine. And most important, it's furry. If you look at each individual silver needle bud, you'll see it is covered in soft, silver fur, which means that you can consume something furry without feeling guilty. It's also fun to say, "My tea is furry."

yerba maté

This is South America's most popular beverage, and for good reason. It has a potent, grassy flavor—almost like oversteeped green tea—with an added subtle tobacco-like flavor. This may not seem like it would be a tempting flavor combination, but it's hearty, full-bodied character is immediately addictive.

Originally introduced by the Guarani Indians of Paraguay and Uruguay, this beverage is brewed from the dried leaves and stemlets of the yerba maté tree, a little tree native to the subtropical highlands of Paraguay, Uruguay, Argentina, and Brazil. Yerba maté is considered to be a stimulant since it has a considerable amount of caffeine (depending on how it's prepared), and is also known to contain lots of antioxidants, to aid in digestion and to be an all-natural appetite suppressant.

However, the coolest part about yerba maté is its accessories. Traditionally, it is almost always made and served out of a gourd (also called a maté) that is usually made out of the hard shell of a local fruit, and it is sipped through a bombilla, a very clever culinary invention that combines a straw with a filter (so minced yerba maté leaves don't reach the mouth). Bombillas are usually made out of metal, basketwork, or perforated wood. And the nicest thing about yerba maté is the tradition of people sharing it. The same maté gourd is usually passed around and enjoyed by many people. Aww . . .

Pu-erh (poo er)

Let's talk about pu-erh, okay? Pu-erh (apart from having a name that would, phonetically speaking, get six-year-olds into trouble) is one of the more interesting members of the black tea family, historically speaking. Pu-erh is a compressed tea, meaning that it is packed into cakes during its production to make it easier to transport. Cake tea is the most ancient form of tea manufacture in China and was even written about in the first known book on tea, published in China, circa A.D. 780. Today, high quality pu-erh is still packed into the traditional cake form in varying diameters and packed in bamboo, but it is also sold in leaf form.

Pu-erh can have a very earthy and sweet taste that many tea drinkers find off-putting, and some would go so far as to say it tastes like dirt. Its distinct taste is due to the fact that the tea is usually fermented twice and then aged for an extended period of time, as long as forty or fifty years, which, needless to say, is a long time. High-quality grades are smooth and pleasant (similar to oolong), while crappy ones are bitter. Many people do actually enjoy its earthy taste and health benefits. It is known to be a digestive and has an insignificant amount of caffeine. I have one friend who likes to drink it after she's been gardening because she wants to feel at one with the soil, and apparently drinking tea that tastes like soil helps her do that. To each his (or her) own.

monkey-picked tea

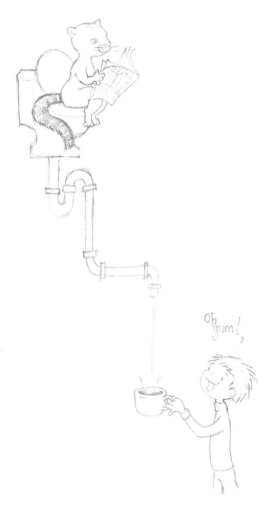

Oh yum!

Yep. You read correctly. Tea picked by monkeys. What else is there to say? Does it taste nice? Yes. Does that matter? No. Why? Because it's picked by monkeys. In China. Why monkeys? a) Monkeys are very cheap labor, b) Having monkeys pick your tea is great, c) The tea that they pick grows in places that are virtually impossible for humans to safely get at, like high cliffs, and d) Monkey-picked tea is way better than boring old human-picked tea.

Now, not all tea that says "monkey-picked tea" is actually picked by monkeys. Sometimes the term simply means high quality, which is ironic, since you wouldn't think that people would consider a beverage that has had monkeys' hands all over it to be high quality. And it's not like you can really wash tea, once it's tea. It pretty much goes from the monkey's hand to your mouth (after some drying and fermenting, of course).

So if you like that sort of thing (partially domesticated animals touching your food and drinks), you might also want to try weasel coffee, which is made from beans that Vietnamese weasels eat and barf up. Yum! Or if that still isn't enough for you, maybe you'd like to try some Indonesian civet coffee, where (oh, you are not going to believe this) the coffee beans have been eaten, partially digested, and then pooed out of a civet cat, and then made into coffee. I know when I look at cat poo I think to myself, "That would make a darn fine cup of joe." But I didn't think anyone else did. Meow!

iced tea

Jasmine pearls

Oh my! The labor that goes into this tea is simply astounding. High-quality, young, green tea leaves (sometimes two different kinds) are carefully chosen. The leaves have to be just right because no one wants to go through this whole process using a tea that is not great. Jasmine flowers are then harvested in the day and set aside in a cool place until night when the flowers become their most fragrant. The tea leaves are then steamed with layers of the oh-so-fragrant jasmine flowers layered over them. Then a small bunch of tea leaves (3 to 5) are tightly hand rolled to about the size of a pearl. Hand rolled. Oh the tedium! Why would one go through this process? Because they look nice, of course. And when the tea unfurls, some of its liquor is emitted slower than other parts of the tea pearl, allowing for multiple infusions.

Though this is not the most common tea ever, it's not difficult to find. Any up-scale tea shop that sells green tea should have jasmine pearls, and it can also be easily found online. And no, it's not exactly cheap, but the fact that these pearls are made from high-quality tea, they are good for multiple infusions. And only about ten of them need to be steeped for one large cup of tea, which makes the price not so bad.

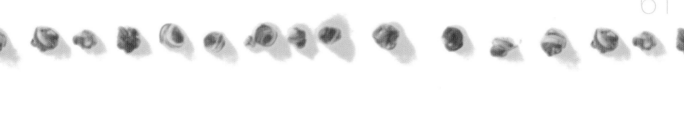

5

Chapter 5: Eat with Your Hands

Kelly will never say it, but the food at teany is amazing. I, on the other hand, can say that the food at teany is amazing because I had nothing to do with its creation. I'm very glad that it exists, and you will be too if you come into teany and/or make any of these sandwiches at home.

—Moby

pan bagna

(aka reason for living)

Oh my gosh! There are no words to describe how unbelievably

good this sandwich is. (Yes, a Pan Bagna is a sandwich.) You don't know this yet, but you bought this book for this recipe. In fact, your parents had you so that you could one day try this sandwich. If you make this sandwich, your life will be richer, more fulfilling, and this world will be an all-around more pleasant place for you to be.

And the really great news is that it is easy to make. And while you could buy olive tapenade at the store, why not make it yourself? It sounds so much more fancy than it really is, and you can impress your friends by asking them if they want extra tapenade on their Pan Bagna.

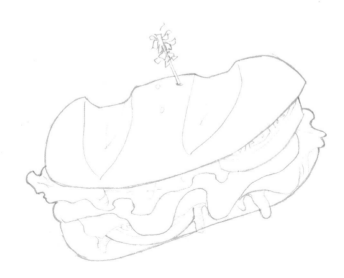

Here are the ingredients you will need to get in order to find heaven on earth:

Olive Tapenade

15 pitted calamata olives (or any other nice black olive)

½ tablespoon olive oil

1 clove garlic

Sandwich

1 long, narrow, crispy loaf of bread (like a French baguette, or my
  favorite, cibatta bread)

½ cup finely chopped red onion

3 vine-ripe or plum tomatoes, sliced
  salt and pepper to taste

1 roasted red and/or yellow pepper (you can get these jarred or
  canned, at any grocery store)

1 small bunch of arugula (well-washed, this stuff is sandy)

1 small bunch of fresh basil leaves

2 tablespoons balsamic vinegar

1½ tablespoon olive oil

Prepare the Olive Tapenade by putting all ingredients into a food processor or blender and blend until somewhat smooth (not too smooth, it shouldn't look like pâté), and you're done. See, wasn't that easy?

Slice the bread the long way, and spread the Olive Tapenade on the bottom layer of bread. Layer the following, in this order: chopped red onion, sliced tomatoes, salt and pepper, red and/or yellow pepper, arugula, and basil.
Drizzle the vinegar on top of the layers of vegetables then drizzle the olive oil on the underside of the other piece of bread. It wouldn't hurt to throw a few sprigs of rosemary into that olive oil a day before using.

Put the sandwich together and press down on it, then wrap it tightly in cling wrap. Place it in the fridge for at least 1 hour, and at most a day. This will let all the flavors marinate and combine to make what I call the best sandwich on earth.

Makes 1 sandwich

Some variations on the Pan Bagna (aka Reason for Living):

Use Simple Pesto (recipe on pg. 81) or Sun-Dried Tomato and White Bean Spread (pg. 19) instead of, or in addition to, the Olive Tapenade.

Add some vegetarian pepperoni slices for a more traditional Pan Bagna.

cashew butter
sandwich

Some people think that the only way to cure a

hangover is to drink more. Others think that aspirin and lots of water do the trick. Still others will actually try Moby's hangover tip (see page 36), and decide that it works. And then there are those people who don't bother thinking about how to get over it and just decide not to challenge the healing process of the body, but simply to feed it with savory, mushy, heavy, salty, sweet, crispy fried foods instead. The cashew butter sandwich is all that and more.

I would suggest making two of these sandwiches for each person eating them, because whoever is eating it will definitely want more than one, and it would be an insult to both the Cashew Butter Sandwich and the person eating it if it was to be served with anything else besides more Cashew Butter Sandwiches.

What you will need in order to enjoy your hangover to the fullest extent:

> Cashew butter, to taste
> Apple butter, to taste
> ½ **to 1** tablespoon pure maple syrup, to taste
> **1** banana
> **4** slices white bread
> Vegan margarine

Cashew Cow
makes
Cashew butter

For each sandwich, slather one slice of bread with cashew butter and the other slice with apple butter. Slice the banana (use a quarter of a banana for each sandwich) and place it on the cashew butter side. Drizzle the maple syrup on the apple butter side. Close the sandwich carefully (you don't want any runaway banana slices) and lightly spread vegan margarine on both sides of the sandwich. Grill until lightly brown. Then enjoy, enjoy, enjoy!

Makes 2 sandwiches and serves 1

PLEASE NOTE: It's not just hungover people who love this sandwich. Everyone seems to—especially kids!

my mom's burrito recipe

(and the birthday meal)

"It's a tea robot, you dimwit," said his cute girlfriend.

"Oh. I knew that," he said. And then they left.

And then they returned. And then we were purchased and wrapped up and transported to the dim-witted bald guy's apartment in the disturbingly gentrified neighborhood of Nolita (which apparently is Italian for "bald yuppie"). We spent a few months living in the bald guy's apartment and then we were transferred to teany, which was to become our new, and apparently permanent, home.

And here we are. And we like it here. It's better than the bald guy's apartment, and it's certainly better than the trunk of the car we were in before the outsider art show. Yes, we like teany. The customers are nice to us. The staff is nice to us. And from 1:00 A.M. until 7:30 A.M. we have the place to ourselves, which is pretty great and affords us the opportunity to plan the eventual overthrow of your puny planet. See, we are clad in metal and have supercomputers for brains, even if we are humble tea robots. Try this on for size, human: "All hail the mighty robots, especially the not-so-mighty, but overall very important, tea robots!" Has a nice ring to it, huh? Welcome to your future, human.

Sincerely Yours,
Tea Robot 1

teany "chicken" salad

(aka the best picnic food ever)

I know, this recipe just begs the question, "What would a bunch of vegetarians make chicken salad out of?" Why, texturized vegetable protein (tvp), of course. Doesn't that sound appetizing? Would you like some twice-baked mineralized yeast base (tbmyb) to go along with that? Just kidding. I don't think there is any such thing as tbmyb. But I am absolutely certain that there is such a thing as tvp, and it's very handy. It pretty much takes on the flavor of whatever you prepare it with, and has the general texture of ground beef. Except it comes from vegetable proteins instead of nice little cows and their proteins.

What you will need in order to create the best picnic food ever:

16 ounces un-chicken broth, or vegetable broth
3 cups texturized vegetable protein (tvp)
1 stalk celery, diced very small
¼ medium onion, diced very small
1 dill pickle spear, diced small
1 tablespoon Dijon mustard
2 tablespoons veganaise
  salt to taste
  pepper to taste
2 teaspoons dried kelp flakes (not imperative, but it does make this fake chicken salad more convincing)

In a medium-sized saucepan, bring the broth to a boil, then add the tvp. Bring the temperature to medium, and allow to cook until nearly all of the liquid is absorbed. Put the tvp in a container and refrigerate until cold (if you're in a rush, spread the mixture in a shallow pan and put it in the freezer for 20 minutes, stirring once after 10 minutes).

Add all other ingredients to the tvp, and mix well. Chicken salad is complete! This salad is best when served on toasted whole grain bread that has been lightly spread with vegan margarine. Greens and tomatoes work great with it too! And if you want to be fancy, as we at teany like to be, serve it open-faced. It can also be served as a generous topping to a salad. And one last thing, watermelon tastes damn good with any chicken salad dish.

Makes 8 servings (which is great because it keeps for at least 5 days)

pesto pizza
with fried zucchini and capers

And by pizza, I don't mean fancy, make-your-own-crust pizza. I mean whatever-is-in-the-pantry pizza. All you need is an oven and a dream (and a reasonably stocked kitchen), and the pizza potential is endless. For crust you can use a French bread loaf, an English muffin, pita bread, crumpets, whatever. I draw the line at pop tarts and doughnuts, but that's just me. Here, we used some day-old focaccia bread, which worked out really well. Then we basically just added what we had around, and came up with something wonderful. The amounts of topping ingredients you use will be based on your pizza bottom. Let your instincts and taste buds guide you.

This is what you'll need in order to achieve Pesto Pizza greatness:

- **2–3** tablespoons canola oil or vegan margarine
- ½ cup water
- **1** teaspoon baking powder
- ½ cup white flour
- ½ tablespoon salt
- ½ tablespoon pepper
- ½ zucchini, cut in half and then sliced very thin (for frying)
- **1 6-inch x 6-inch** slice foccacia bread
- **2** tablespoons Simple Pesto (see recipe on page 87)
- **8** sun-dried tomatoes, julienned
- **1** tablespoon capers

Warm the oil or margarine in a frying pan on medium-high heat. In a bowl, mix together water, baking powder, flour, and salt and pepper. Dip the slices of zucchini in the mix, and place in pan with hot oil. Fry until crisp, then lay out on paper towels and dab the tops to remove excess oil. Spread the pesto generously on your pizza bottom (the harder the pizza bottom is, the more pesto you should add). Lay the fried zucchini strips on the pizza evenly, then sprinkle with the sun-dried tomato pieces and capers. Add a little more salt and pepper, and bake in the oven at 375˚ F. for 5 minutes, or until pizza bottom is a little bit crispy.

Makes 2 servings

simple pesto

Normally pesto has cheese in it. For those who don't eat cheese, it's nearly impossible to find a dairy-free pesto. And do you want to know a little pesto secret? It doesn't taste any different when it doesn't have cheese. And do you want to know another little pesto secret? It is so easy to make, doesn't require any serious cooking skills, and takes about two seconds. All you need to know is how to work a food processor, and how to get the sand off your basil (you filthy, sandy-basil lover, you).

What you'll need for your simple, I-can't-believe-there's-no-parmesan pesto recipe:

½ cup extra virgin olive oil

3 tablespoons pine nuts

3 cups washed basil leaves, off their stems

1 garlic clove, minced

salt to taste

Heat 1 tablespoon of the olive oil in a small frying pan on low heat, and lightly toast the pine nuts. Then throw all ingredients, including the rest of the oil and the toasted pine nuts, into a food processor and mix until all is smooth but not too smooth. There should still be little pine nut chunks.

Now, what to do with your pesto? You can toss it into some pasta, or make bruscetta, or mix it into a nice vegetable and bean soup. I like to use it as a pizza sauce. So take a look at the Pesto Pizza with Fried Zucchini and Capers recipe on pages 79 and 80.

Makes 1½ cups

Chapter 6: Cold Drinks for Hot People

We opened teany in the summer, and we learned pretty quickly that the market for piping hot tea isn't exactly huge when it's 130 degrees outside and the sidewalks are melting. So to better serve our friends and neighbors (and so as to not go out of business), we invented a bunch of lovely cold and iced beverages.

teany antioxidant cooler

I give full credit for this teany best seller to Moby. He said, "Let's make a drink that's got a ton of antioxidants in it," and I said, 'No one will want that." But we went ahead and made it, put in on the menu, and wouldn't you know it, it's our most popular iced drink. So once again, Moby was right. And in case you all didn't know why antioxidants are so good, it's because they help prevent cancer and do a bunch of other fantastic things for you as well. So get your hands on some white tea, and make yourself, and all your loved ones, the Teany Antioxidant Cooler.

What you will need in order to make our best seller at home:

> **3** parts white tea
> **1** part pomegranate juice
> **1** part blueberry juice
> **1** part pear (preferably) or apple juice

Half of this drink is iced white tea. Any kind. I would suggest getting a nice high-quality, loose-leaf kind like silver needle or white peony, but whatever you can find will do. Just make sure that whatever kind you get, you let it steep for at least 10 minutes to get most of its antioxidant properties.

The other half is equal parts pomagranate juice, blueberry juice, and pear or apple juice. Mix well using the ratios suggested, pour over ice, and enjoy!

Makes as much as you want

teany red cooler

This is the first tea/juice mixture that Moby and I ever invented. Actually, Moby invented it, and I just sorta cleaned up the mess. This is an excellent palate-cleansing drink to go with the Pan Bagnia, or any Mediterranean-flavored dish, and the most perfect spring and summer beverage, next to the teany Lavender Lemonade (featured on the next page), of course.

You will need equal parts of:

> **mint tea**
> **any black tea** that has been flavored with a red tart and sweet fruit: plum or raspberry; black tea works best, we think
> **cranberry juice**

You can make this recipe in any quantity, because it calls for equal parts of all three ingredients. Steep the mint tea for 5 to 10 minutes. You want to make the tea very strong, and you don't have to worry about it turning bitter because it's herbal. Steep the black tea for 3 minutes, and no longer, because it will turn the whole mixture bitter. Pour equal parts of all three liquids into a container and refrigerate. Garnish with fresh mint leaves if you are feeling fancy.

Makes as much as you want

lavender lemonade

Chapter 7: Some of Our Friends
(we don't actually know these people)

There would be no teany without teany patrons. I like the word "patron" because it reminds me of a Central American ranch owner. Owning teany is kind of like being a Central American ranch owner. Well, no it's not. Anyway, here are some interesting facts about our teany patrons.

teany questionaire

DATE

TITLE

Slide•Saver
#7000 • Made in U.S.A.

MUSEUM QUALITY
vue-all®
ARCHIVAL

Though the food, drinks, and ambiance are all great things about teany, what makes teany so special are the people who come here. Really, truly, honestly, we could not have asked for a nicer, funnier, smarter, sweeter clientele. And because this is our best feature, we wanted to show it off in the book ('it' being our super great customers), so we decided to ask a few random teany customers some fun questions and take their pictures. Here are some of the results of our goofy teany questionaire, answered by very good sports.

Q: What brought you to teany?

Caffeine fix
Blind adoration
Tea party
I come most days. It's part of
my attempt at stability.

Q: What is your favoite thing
about teany?

Board games
Teas
The decor
Teany chef salad
The animated pics of vegetables
on the bathroom walls
Strawberry shortcake
Good music
The clock with the baby chicken
That it's drenched in sunlight

Q: If you were a drink, what kind of
drink would you be?

Southern-style sweet tea (the
way my mama makes it)
A good shot of tequila
Green tea
Vanilla chai
Teanychino
Tincture of opium mixed with a
chocolate shake
A smoothie because I'm smoov

Q: First artist whose record or
soundtrack you bought?

Olivia Newton-John
Public Enemy
Flashdance Soundtrack
Queen
Culture Club
Run DMC
Cyndi Lauper

Q: What was the first concert you ever went to?

Duran Duran
Debbie Gibson
Judas Priest
Journey
New Kids on the Block

Q: If you were president, what would you do in your fiirst day in office?

Hire Bill Clinton as my adviser
Take a day off at my ranch in Texas
Forgive student loans
Write letters of apology to at least 100 countries
Set up all of my desk accessories
Test the kitchen out: eat a lot of BBQ and Cajun food

Q: Would you rather be a seal or a buzzard? (Remember, buzzards may be ugly and eat dead gross things, but seals get clubbed. Choose wisely.)

The seals won. Twenty-two teany customers out of 30 would rather be cute, lie on rocks with all their seal friends, and risk getting clubbed than be ugly but get to fly and have a steady food supply. Hmmm.

It's a fact! 2/3 teany customers would rather go back in time than go to the moon!

21 teany customers would rather go back in time 100 years while only 9 teany customers want to see the future 100 years from now.

Q: Would you rather have a house full of spider monkeys, spider plants, or spiders?

Only 13 terany customers out of 30 would want a house full of spider monkeys! Isn't that nuts? Wouldn't you automatically think that EVERYONE would want a house full of spider monkeys? I'm truly shocked. And also to my surprise, 5 people actually chose spiders, leaving 18 mature and logical individuals who chose spider plants.

Q: We then asked a riddle: What would you have if all the cars in the nation were pink? (HINT: switch some words.)

Ten people got the joke, but I witnessed three people cheat off their friends. So, seven people got the joke. If you want to know the answer, you will have to turn the book upside down and look at the bottom of the page.

Q: How appealing is it to you to live like a baby for a week? (You'd get rolled around in a stroller, get carried everywhere, poo in a diaper, get spoon-fed, and basically live like a king?)

11 people chose "not at all, I have respect for myself"

6 people chose "maybe just a little bit"

4 people chose "who knows? It's only a week, why not try it?"

1 person chose "well, it would be nice to not have to lift a finger or worry about a thing…"

9 people chose "where's my crib?"

Isn't this a no-brainer? I (Kelly) am absolutely, genuinely shocked that all of those questioned would not jump at the chance to live like a baby for a week in diapers and all. But then again, I wrote this question, and only someone who really wants to live like a baby for a week could ever think of it. Turns out more people have respect for themselves (and certainly more than I have for myself) than I thought.

Answer: a pink carnation! HA!

T.

by Dimitri Ehrlich

Some think that they will never see

a poem as lovely as a tree

and while I'd love to just agree

(there's nothing wrong with forestry)

I can easily list, like, twenty-three

things I prefer to shrubbery

some favorite stuff—and this is just me:

1. Those little towels marked he and she.

2. When Hank Bendelman became Bendel, Henri.

3. Total domination at a spelling bee.

4. When B-boys call each other "G."

5. A good escape hatch and time to flee.

6. A few cold grapes and a hunk of rennet-free vegan soy Brie.

7. A really long-ass winning spree.

8. The opposable thumb and index, and a functioning knee.

This is a poem from our friend Dimitri. He is superhuman. Really. He does five hours of martial arts a day and is a great writer and is the funniest person we know, and yet he still finds time to drink vodka and practice Buddhism and stay abreast of disturbing anti-Zionist conspiracies.

9. Certain Civil War heroes, such as Robert E. Lee.

10. Stuff that's cheap, marked down, or free.

11. Hearing French girls say, "Mais oui."

12. My karate uniform, known in Japanese as a "gee."

13. Un-pear-like torsos shaped like a *V*.

14. For whom bells toll (the answer's thee).

15. Apartment brokers who charge no fee.

16. The way Scottish people call small things "wee."

17. These colors: burnt sienna, raw ochre, and toasted pea.

18. A sudden burst of senseless glee.

19. A weathered cottage near the sea.

20. The prefixes *ante* and *pre*.

21. Knowing how to simply be.

22. The day they ban the SUV.

23. A place to get the perfect cup of tea.

the first rule of teany

Teany prides itself on being a fairly relaxed and flexible place, but we do have some rigid rules that are almost never broken. Okay, the truth is that we only have one real rule (some of the other quasi rules are actually more like guidelines) and that rule is as follows: Moby's (aka my) music shall never be played in teany. Why is this a rule at teany? Well, because playing my music in teany would just seem to be kind of, I don't know, creepy?

See, I've been in the situation where I'm out being social and one of my songs comes on and it invariably makes me feel very self-conscious. Don't get me wrong. I enjoy my own music. I just don't really like hearing it in social situations, primarily because it suddenly makes me deconstruct whichever piece of my music happens to be playing and then I'm suddenly asking myself, "Could I have mixed the drums better?" or, "That keyboard part isn't very good," or "Should I have added more high-end in mastering?" etc.

And another reason that we don't ever play my music in teany is that we never wanted teany to be a "celebrity-owned" restaurant. Most "celebrity-owned" restaurants tend to be big, fancy, flashy places (which is fine), but we always wanted teany to be little and cute and autonomous. I'm proud to be one of the two people who owns teany, but I always wanted my ownership to be a subtle thing (i.e., teany: owned by Kelly Tisdale and Moby) as opposed to an unsubtle thing (i.e., MOBY owns teany, along with Kelly Tisdale). Does this make any sense? I guess it's just me, in a long-winded way, trying to explain our rule about never playing my music in teany.

—Moby

afternoon playlist

Buddy Holly—**Buddy Holly: Greatest Hits**
Calexico—**Convict Pool**
Squeeze—**Singles 45's and Under**
Felt—**Strange Idols Pattern & Other Short Stories**
Neil Diamond—**The Essential Neil Diamond**
Blur—**Blur**
Love—**Love Story 1966–1972**
Roy Orbison—**The All-Time Greatest Hits of Roy Orbison**
Adam Ant—**Antics in the Forbidden Zone**
The Shins—**Chutes Too Narrow**
Magnetic Fields—**69 Love Songs**
Pulp—**His n' Hers**
The Modern Lovers—**The Modern Lovers**
Billy Idol—**Rebel Yell**

The afternoon playlist is all about keeping people's heads bopping, giving them a little midday energy to carry them through with the rest of their day. Like the morning playlist, these albums aren't going to shock or ruin one's mood. They're just good solid tunes, with a fair amount of energy. Like caffeine for the ears.

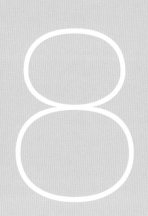

Chapter 8: Eat with Your Fork

Now we get serious. Kelly is a gifted foodmaker (I like inventing germanically long anglo words), and one of my favorite things is being able to sit back and sample the fruits (not literal fruits, although literal fruit can be nice too) of her labor. If you make any of these recipes at home, feel free to invite me over to sample the fruits of your labor because I really like to eat.

—Moby

asian vegetable and noodle salad with spicy peanut sauce

I've always been a little intimidated by the idea of trying to make authentic Asian food because I didn't grow up Asian and therefore figured I was going to screw it up. Then I realized that with this whole Asian fusion thing being so popular that under the guise of "experimentation," I couldn't really screw anything up. I figured that as long as it had noodles; crispy, raw vegetables; some spice; and some crushed peanuts, it couldn't be bad. And I was right! This recipe is not so bad. It's so not bad that it's actually very good, if I do say so myself.

What you will need in order to make this so-not-bad-it's-actually-very-good Asian salad:

Spicy Peanut Sauce:

4 tablespoons Asian chili sauce

2 tablespoons peanut butter

2 tablespoons grated ginger juice (just grate some ginger and squeeze the juice out)

2 tablespoons sesame oil

4 teaspoons soy sauce

2 teaspoons rice vinegar

2 tablespoons lemon juice

2 cloves finely chopped garlic

Salad

11 ounces dried soba noodles

4 large carrots, julienned

16 sugar snap peas, julienned

2 cups shredded red cabbage

1 tablespoon chopped green onions

2 tablespoons sesame oil

4 tablespoons crushed peanuts

To prepare the peanut sauce, put all ingredients into a bowl and whisk. Easy.

Next, to prepare the salad, boil the soba noodles until al dente. Throw the carrots, snap peas, red cabbage, and green onions in the spicy peanut sauce, mix well, and set aside. Toss the noodles with the sesame oil. They should be a little slippery but not drenched.

To serve, put the noodles in the bottom of individual bowls, add the vegetable mix on top, and sprinkle each serving with a tablespoon of crushed peanuts.

Makes 4 main course servings

avocado, beet, and mango, salad with blood orange tea vinaigrette

(aka dish of bliss)

Why is this the dish of bliss? Can you think of a better way to describe a salad that is savory, sweet, crunchy, mushy, fresh, filling, and really pretty? And you aren't making just any dressing for this salad either. People come to teany just for this dressing. We serve it on every salad, and our customers just can't seem to get enough of it. In case you want to stray from perfection, you can use any kind of herbal orange tea for the dressing. But the blood orange tea is especially nice because it's a little bit sweeter and richer in its orange flavor.

When making this recipe, keep in mind that there will be plenty left for future salads (20 servings to be exact). It stores well in the fridge, but must be taken out an hour before serving and mixed because it separates and solidifies.

HINT: If you've never peeled and cubed a mango before, you're in for a special treat! Let's just say, you may want to get two mangos instead of one. On your first attempt, you will most likely end up slaughtering the poor fruit, leaving mango flesh everywhere but in the bowl, with the end result nothing like the oh-so-desirable shape of a cube. However, once you've had some practice, the second time should be the charm.

To prepare this savory, sweet, crunchy, mushy, lovely dish of bliss you will need the following:

Blood Orange Tea Vinaigrette

1 cup white wine vinegar

1 tablespoon blood orange tea

1 teaspoon salt

1 teaspoon garlic, very finely chopped

1 tablespoon sugar

1 tablespoon Dijon mustard

1 cup olive oil

Salad

2 avocados

1 mango

12-ounce can of beets

¼ cup crushed walnuts

   oak leaf lettuce (optional)

To Prepare Blood Orange Tea Vinaigrette

The first step to making this delicious vinaigrette is to prepare the blood orange vinegar by mixing the wine vinegar with blood orange tea. Put the vinegar and loose tea in a small pot and bring to a boil, uncovered. Turn the heat off and allow to cool. Once cooled, strain the blood orange vinegar until all the tea pieces are out. You should be left with just about ¼ cup of vinegar.

Mix ¼ cup of the blood orange vinegar with the salt, garlic, sugar, and mustard. Whisk until blended. While continuing to whisk, drizzle in the olive oil until completely blended. If you have extra vinegar left over, you can add more if you want a stronger blood orange taste.

To Prepare the Salad

Peel the avocados and mango. Cut the avocados, mango, and beets into bite-sized cubes. Mix with the walnuts and vinaigrette, stirring the mixture gently. Serve immediately (or sometime before the avocados go brown) as a side dish or over a bed of oak leaf lettuce as a main course.

Makes 4 servings

three dishes loosely based on indian cuisine

(curried potatoes and peas, coconut-creamed spinach, jasmine and green tea rice)

This may seem like a vague title, but I swear, this was well

thought out. Why only "loosely based?" Well, I don't claim to be an expert on Indian cuisine, and I don't want some Indian food expert coming to me saying that I have no idea what I'm talking about. However, I'm a huge fan of Indian food, which Moby initially introduced me to and which we would eat whenever we wanted to go out for greasy food and he didn't want to leave his three-block radius. And to be fair, why should he? The most amazing vegetarian Indian restaurants in the city, if not the state, or the country, are a stone's throw from his home in the East Village.

These truly amazing dishes are what my little taste buds learned from. So when I was creating these dishes, I had a lot of sensory knowledge to go on, even though, as I said before, I'm no expert. I just know that these dishes are delicious. If you can't get amazing Indian food where you are (or are just feeling crafty) don't walk, run (!) to your nearest grocery store and get yourself some curry! And all the other things that these recipes call for!

Curried Potatoes and Peas

¾ pound peeled potatoes, cut into bite-sized pieces

1½ teaspoons salt

1½ teaspoons curry powder

½ teaspoon ground cumin

½ teaspoon ground coriander

2 tablespoons olive oil

1 small yellow onion, chopped small

2 garlic cloves, very finely chopped or mashed

1 cup frozen peas

½ cup coconut milk

Coconut Creamed Spinach

1 pound spinach

⅔ cup coconut milk

¼ cup silken tofu

2 tablespoons vegan margarine

2 teaspoons ground cumin

  salt and pepper to taste

Jasmine and Green Tea Rice

2 cups water

1½ tablespoons green tea leaves (you can boost the jasmineness

  of the rice by using jasmine green tea)

1 cup jasmine rice

1 teaspoon salt

To Prepare Curried Potatoes and Peas

Boil potatoes until completely soft. In a separate bowl, combine salt, curry, cumin, and coriander, and set aside. Heat the oil in a skillet at medium-high heat. Then add the onions, and cook until they are translucent. Add the spice mix, as well as the garlic, to the onions and cook for 2 minutes. Add the potatoes and peas. Stir gently for 5 minutes. Add coconut milk, and stir until mixture is evenly coated. Have a taste, so you know how good it is, but exert some self-control and wait until the spinach and rice dishes are completed. Trust me on this.

To Prepare Coconut Creamed Spinach

Chop the spinach, then steam over boiling water until it's completely wilted. Put the steamed spinach in a colander and press out the excess liquid and set aside. Put coconut milk, silken tofu, and margarine into a food processor and blend until mixture is smooth. Heat the coconut milk mixture in a saucepan, and add the spinach, cumin, salt and pepper, and simmer on low to medium heat for 5 minutes, stirring the whole time. Again, have a taste, be in heaven for a moment, and hold off until the rice dish is done. (I'm not trying to tease you, really. I have your best interest at heart!)

To Prepare Jasmine and Green Tea Rice

Bring two cups of water to a boil and add the green tea. Allow to steep for 4 minutes. Strain the water, discarding the tea leaves and saving the water. Combine the liquid with the rice and salt, and bring the liquid to a boil. Once it's boiling, reduce heat to medium, cover the pan, and let simmer until the rice is tender and all the liquid is absorbed.

To Serve

Now, you may feast! These three dishes should all go on the same plate in equal amounts (like the picture). Do not treat the jasmine rice like crappy boil-in-bag rice. It's yummy as a separate starch and should not have more dominating dishes piled on top of it.

Makes 4 entree-sized servings

Okay, so now that it is in this book, the recipe isn't top secret anymore. But once upon a time, teany chili fanatics nearly beat down the teany door for this recipe. They sent in spies. They kidnapped our chef and held her for recipe ransom! Okay, that is not the truth, but I'm sure they were plotting something. But I assure you, we spent years guarding this top-secret recipe with our lives and, to be honest, we're tired. And now we realize that we were foolish. We have realized that the world would be a better place if it knew that the key ingredients for making the world's best chili might have something to do with (drumroll please) cocoa, espresso, and cashews . . .

The ingredients you will need in order to make teany's not-so-secret Top-Secret Chili are as follows:

¾ cup olive oil

2 cups diced onions

¼ cup chopped garlic

8 ounces regular-flavored seitan, sliced in bite-sized pieces

¾ cup red chopped peppers

¾ cup green chopped peppers

1 tablespoon ground cumin

⅛ cup chili pepper

½ tablespoon crushed red chili peppers

1 tablespoon chili powder

⅛ cup cocoa powder

½ shot espresso or ¼ cup strong coffee

4 cups crushed tomatoes with liquid

½ cup chopped cashews

2 cups kidney beans

2 cups white beans

1 cup corn (can be fresh, frozen, or canned)

salt and pepper to taste

vegan sour cream (try tofutti sour cream), to taste

In a large stockpot (1 gallon), heat ¾ cup olive oil. When the oil is hot, add the onions and cook until they are translucent (about 3 or 4 minutes). Add the garlic and sauté for 1 minute. Add the seitan and sauté for 2 minutes, then add the red and green peppers. Cook for 2 minutes, and then add cumin, chili pepper, crushed red chili peppers, chili powder, cocoa powder, and espresso or coffee. Allow the spices to cook for 5 minutes, stirring constantly, and then add the crushed tomatoes and cashews. Once the mix is simmering, add the kidney beans, white beans, corn, salt, and pepper. Let the chili simmer on medium-low heat until some of the liquid has evaporated and the chili is nice and thick (approximately 1 hour). Top off each serving with a dollop of vegan sour cream.

Makes 6 servings˙

˙VERY PROFESSIONAL COOK'S NOTE: Make this dish at least once before you invite your friends over to share it with you be- cause once you try it, you may realize that you don't want to share it. When I make this chili, I tell no one.

rich and creamy vodka sauce

For those of you who don't know what vodka sauce is, the best way to describe it is to say that it is a sauce sent from the gods. Traditional vodka sauce is a thin (not very chunky) herb-filled tomato sauce with heavy cream and the tang of vodka or wine. Heavy, creamy, heavenly goodness! I could consume a vodka sauce dish for breakfast, lunch, and dinner every day and be the happiest girl on the planet. However, heavy cream consumed with this frequency would give anyone a heart attack, so I invented this dairy-free recipe to save my life and to improve yours. This recipe takes no time and is excellent as a sauce for pizza or for ziti.

⅓ cup silken tofu
10 kalmata olives, pitted
2 cups jarred tomato sauce
2 tablespoons vegan margarine
1 tablespoon white cooking sherry

Throw all ingredients into a food processor and blend until smooth. Heat on stovetop or in microwave, and pour over your favorite pasta. You can also spread it onto pizza dough and add your favorite toppings, or keep it simple and add just a few basil leaves. Expect an uncontrollable and overwhelming outpouring of gratitude to burst from your taste buds directly up to the heavens, or Little Italy, depending on your beliefs.

Makes 4 servings if used as a pasta sauce

teany middle eastern plate
(hummus, tabouleh, lentil salad, and hot sauce)

Our teany Middle Eastern Plate is made of three traditional dishes— hummus, tabouleh, and lentil salad with our own special flavors thrown in. Having had more than a few Middle Eastern plates in my life, I am pretty confident that I am not the only one who a) is sick of conventional hummus, b) is bummed out when the tabouleh I order always seems to look so much better than it tastes, and c) would rather have a lentil salad than baba ghanoush (okay, maybe I am just prejudiced against eggplant, but bear with me).

So we are here to reinvent the traditional Middle Eastern plate our own teany way. There's no doubt about it, hummus is some tasty stuff. However, since it is available everywhere and since it is so easy to make, I feel like maybe a few of us have overdone it with the hummus. If you are experiencing hummus burnout, this recipe is going to make you love it like you loved conventional hummus the first two hundred times you had it. We also created a tabouleh that's so yummie you will throw the pita bread over your shoulder and find the largest spoon you can to shovel piles of this most perfect crunchy, herby, tangy salad into your super-psyched mouth. And while traditionally baba ghanoush would be on a Middle Eastern plate, eggplant is my least favorite vegetable that exists. Hey! Just because I'm a vegetarian, that doesn't mean I have to like every vegetable on the planet! I mean, Moby's a vegan, and he doesn't like cauliflower or zucchini or summer squash! However, we both think that lentils are dandy, so when we have this Middle Eastern plate, we make an incredible lentil salad instead.

And If you go so far as to make the three dishes here for teany's version of the Middle Eastern plate, you may as well take it all the way and make the hot sauce too. This recipe is especially fun to make when you're upset because you can grind out your tension with a mortar and pestle. And if you are secretly mad at someone who will be eating this dish later, add two jalepeño chilis instead of one!

What you will need in order to breathe new life into this traditional dish:

Hummus

16 ounces chick peas

⅓ cup tahini

3 tablespoons lemon juice

1 clove garlic

1 teaspoon fresh oregano

2 roasted red peppers

salt and pepper to taste

2 tablespoons roasted pine nuts (you can buy them raw and put

them in a pan on low to medium heat until they start to

get brown and really oily)

Tabouleh

1 cup of quinoa'

2 cups cold water

2 ripe tomatoes, skinned, seeded, and chopped

½ cucumber, seeded and diced

1 clove garlic, minced

3 scallions, diced

1 cup chopped parsley

¼ cup of mint, minced

4 tablespoon lemon juice

juice from a quarter of one lime

2 tablespoons extra virgin olive oil

salt and pepper to taste

Lentil salad

1 cup French lentils

2 cups water

½ cup sliced almonds

1 cup whole green beans

1 tablespoon walnut oil

½ tablespoon lemon juice

1 clove crushed garlic

Hot Sauce (or sweet revenge)

4 garlic cloves

⅓ cup parsley, finely minced

⅓ cup cilantro, finely minced

1 jalapeno chili, seeded

⅓ cup extra virgin olive oil

3 tablespoons lemon juice

½ teaspoon ground cumin

½ teaspoon ground coriander

⅓ teaspoon cayenne

salt to taste

quinoa is available at any decent health food store, where all the other grains are sold. This grain is light and fluffy, with a slight crunch and a nutty flavor. It is also one of the only naturally occurring foods available to vegetarians that contains all amino acids. Good stuff.

To Make the Hummus

Throw all ingredients—except for 1 of the 2 tablespoons of roasted pine nuts—into a food processor. Process until smooth (not toothpaste smooth, it should still have some texture). Sprinkle the other tablespoon of pine nuts on top of the hummus as a garnish before serving.

To Make the Tabouleh

Put the quinoa in 2 cups of cold water in a medium-sized saucepan, and cook on high heat until it boils. Turn the heat down to low, and let the quinoa cook until all the water is absorbed. Chill the quinoa in a freezer for 20 minutes. Skin the tomatoes by dropping them in boiling water for 5 seconds or until the skin starts to peel. Take the tomatoes out and peel them; the skin should fall right off. Chop or mince cucumber, garlic, scallions, parsley, and mint accordingly. Add lemon and lime juice, olive oil, salt, and pepper and stir gently until the mixture is even.

To Make Lentil Salad

Put the lentils in a small pot with 2 cups of water. Bring the lentils to a boil, then turn the heat down low so they simmer for 6 to 8 minutes until they are soft, but not mushy.

Drain the lentils and rinse them under cold water. Heat the almonds and green beans in a pan on low to medium heat until the almonds are very dark and toasty, but not burned. Add the lentils, walnut oil, lemon juice, and garlic, and gently stir until completely mixed.

To Make the Hot Sauce

In a mortar, grind the garlic vigorously into a paste with the pestle. Then add the parsley and cilantro, and grind more. Then the jalapeno, and grind more! Then add the rest of the ingredients and grind even more, until you've released every ounce of anger in you, or until the sauce has a thin but chunky texture. Use this sauce lightly (or serve on the side), it's powerful stuff.

NOTE: You can also use a blender for this recipe if you don't have a mortar, but be very careful not to overblend. It should be chunky, not pureed.

To Serve

I would suggest serving these three salads with toasted pita bread (unless you would rather shovel all these nice salads directly into your mouth with a large spoon). All you have to do is put pita bread in the oven (or toaster oven) for 2 to 3 minutes, at 350° F. When you take it out, it will still be soft, but let it sit for a minute, and it will soon become crunchy. If you want to be super fancy, brush one side of the pita lighty with any kind of oil before putting it in the oven, so it's even crispier. Break apart the enormous pita chip, and dip!

If you make the whole Middle Eastern Plate, it comes out to be a lot of food. But don't worry, all of the dishes can sit in the fridge for at least a day. Even better: It's the perfect dinner party meal.

Makes 6 entree-sized servings

french toast with plum syrup

On the cover of this book, we promised romance. So here goes: when Moby and I first began dating, he would make pancakes for breakfast (that's the first romantic part). His recipe for pancakes was very simple. And plain. And bland. But I ate them for years (that's the other romantic part, I guess). And he liked them, so there was no way for him to know that I didn't like them—until I told him two years later. I wouldn't say he was crushed to hear how much I didn't like them, but he was a little perplexed as to why I didn't tell him sooner. The truth is, no one ever made me breakfast before! So then to make it up to him, I told him I was going to make him waffles, egg free of course, since Moby doesn't eat eggs. So I got a waffle iron and a recipe, and with all the cockiness in the world, began to make him waffles. Little did I know that vegan waffles aren't the easiest things to prepare, especially not the first time. So we went out to breakfast that morning.

Why am I telling this story, besides to fulfill the promise of romance made on the cover of this book? Because I learned that out of all the breakfasty things that one would want to pour syrup over (that are also egg free), French Toast is definitely the easiest one to make, with the best results.

To top off this delicious French Toast, we have Plum Syrup. Doesn't Plum Syrup sound like something out of a fairy tale or nursery rhyme? I'm pretty sure that Miss Muffet would definitely have liked some Plum Syrup to go with her curds and whey. Too bad for Miss Muffet because this syrup is worthy of myth and legend.

What you'll need in order to make your sweetheart wake up with a smile on his/her face:

Plum Syrup

3 plums

⅔ cup maple syrup

⅔ cup pear juice (apple juice will do if you can't find pear juice)

½ teaspoon cinnamon

½ teaspoon vanilla extract

1 pinch black pepper

French Toast

2 teaspoons flax seeds, ground

2 teaspoons water

⅔ cup almond milk (soy milk is acceptable too)

1⅓ tablespoons cinnamon

2 teaspoons vanilla extract

2 tablespoons vegan margarine

6 white bread slices, preferably thin

    powdered sugar for garnish (optional)

To make syrup

Stem and pit the plums and cut each into quarters. Combine all ingredients in a food processor and mix until the plum pieces are pureed. Put mixture into a saucepan, and bring to a boil. Then turn the heat to low, cover, and simmer for 15 minutes or until sauce is thick. Strain the syrup in a fine mesh strainer, and fairy-tale syrup is complete! Syrup is best when served warm.

To make French Toast

Whisk flax seeds with water and whisk until foamy (this is the egg substitute, by the way). Add the almond milk, cinnamon, and vanilla extract to the flax and mix. Soak the bread in the liquid mixture. Heat a pan over medium heat and melt the margarine. Panfry the bread until crispy on both sides. Garnish with powdered sugar, and serve with Plum Syrup.

Makes 6 pieces

9

Chapter 9: Herbal Tea Is for Wussies (like us)

Okay, that might sound harsh. We all like herbal tea. It's good for you, and it has no caffeine. So ignore us when we say that "herbal tea is for wussies." We're just trying to sound tough.

peppermint

Oh, the lovely mint plant. Where would we be without it? What would we freshen our breath with? What would take its place in our lovely little herb gardens? What would we put in our mojitos? It frightens me to think of where we would be without it. Especially when you know that if you make tea out of it, it will prevent flatulence. I mean, seriously, any herb that is going to make my breath smell nice and is going to prevent me from having gas half-way through a date is all right with me. A little peppermint tea after a meal that would otherwise end up being, um, explosive, could really save the day.

Besides preventing embarrassing body odors on dates, peppermint also eases nausea and motion sickness, improves digestion, controls muscle aches, and reduces the severity of herpes (not that I, uh, would ever need that or anything, but you know, maybe if you know someone who might, uh, have herpes, you can, uh, tell them about peppermint . . .).

You can even grow your own to make tea out of! Peppermint is so hearty it will grow like a weed if you just plant it, water it, expose it to sun even just a little bit, and occasionally prance around it naked. Then all you have to do is dry it out! And that's really simple: Put the leaves in a container with the lid off, but make sure that all the leaves are completely exposed to the air (otherwise you'll have a peppermint compost pile) and that the container is kept in an area that isn't damp. You'll have dried leaves in less than a week. Then you can infuse dry whole leaves, or break up the leaves, which will emit more liquor, allowing you to use less. Let the peppermint leaves, whole or broken, steep for at least 5 minutes in near-boiling water before drinking.

red peony rosettes and green sea anemones

This tea is named more for the shape of the tea than the tea itself. Both tea rosettes and anemones are made by shaping and hand tying tea leaves—black, oolong, green, or white—of the same length so that when you drop them into hot water, they take the shape of their namesakes. And why would one want to do this to their tea? Basically, because they are really nice to look at. They are really pretty when steeped. Also, they are perfect if you like full-leaf teas or if you want to take your tea on the go because the leaves are all bound together and sit at the bottom of your cup or thermos, so you don't have to bother with a filter or strainer. Also, because the quality of the tea used is always high, and because some of the leaves take longer to unfurl, due to the way they are tied; these are good for multiple steepings. Beauty, function, convenience. This is definitely the tea of the future (of course, the smart and patient Chinese people just happen to have been hand tying for, like, hundreds of years). You can find these hand-tied teas at any high-quality tea shop or online, and they make excellent gifts because they are so precious and pretty.

lavender

Lavender has been a part of human civilization for almost as long as there's been a human civilization. Its use is documented in the Bible (supposedly Adam and Eve brought it with them when they left the Garden of Eden, but that's more apocryphal . . .), and even the ancient Egyptians used it in rituals and embalming.

It's a pretty remarkable herb because, on one hand, it's very hearty (Moby grows it on his roof, and it's always the last of the herbs to give up the ghost in winter), but yet it's known for its delicate scent and soothing properties. It's widely purported to calm nerves, soothe anxiety, and alleviate headaches. And it smells fantastic. And it makes for a really nice infusion. At teany, we infuse lavender heads in boiled water and let them steep for 6 or 7 minutes, and it makes a really nice, calming, purple-ish herbal tea. We also make a Lavender Lemonade that is, if we do say so ourselves, great (see page 86).

hibiscus

Hibiscus is another herb that has been used for thousands of years. Okay, it's not really an herb, it's a flower. In fact, hibiscus has been nicknamed Chinese rose. It's native to Asia and the South Seas, and it's been used as a cooling (and warming) drink by many cultures, from Europeans to Africans to Asians to Americans. Some historians believe that hibiscus infusion was a royal drink of the pharaohs, but it didn't show up in the West until the eighteenth century.

Hibiscus is very tart and bracing, and it makes for a bright red infusion that usually needs to be sweetened to cut its sharpness a bit. There's some debate as to whether hibiscus has health-giving properties, but it's red and its taste is puckery and distinctive, so even if it's not going to help you live forever, it still makes a nice herbal drink.

rooibos

Is there a healthier herbal tea than this? I don't think so. In fact, this herbal tea might rival regular tea in health benefits. Antioxidants? Check. Vitamin C? Check. Everything else your body could ever possibly need? Check. Or almost.

"Rooibos" means "red bush" in Afrikaans. The red bush is actually a shrub with fine needle-like leaves that grows only in the mountains of the western cape in South Africa. The leaves from the bush are bruised, wetted, rolled, spread out, left to ferment, and, finally, air-dried or sun-dried. This herbal tea (the bush comes from the legume family) is vitamin and mineral rich, containing vitamin C, copper, iron, potassium, calcium, fluoride, zinc, manganese, and magnesium. It also contains alpha hydroxy, which is great for the skin (see Rooibos Dry Skin Treatment on page 51). Rooibos has been shown to help treat a number of health problems, including insomnia, irritability, headaches, nervous tension, hypertension, allergies, asthma, and colic in babies. As if that's not enough, it contains antioxidants and has no caffeine.

Basically, you shouldn't be living without this tea. It's also the best herbal substitute for black tea that there is, and is oftentimes consumed by tea fans who don't want the caffeine. And you can mix it with almost anything, and it will taste wonderful. Well, not anything, I wouldn't go mixing rooibos tea with olives, or anything like that, but dried berries, yerba maté, rosehips, dried mango, spices (rooibos chai is very nice!) all work really well. It's amazing iced too, and unlike regular tea, this tea never goes bitter, so you don't have to worry about over steeping it or it becoming acidic.

10

Chapter 10: The Shortest Chapter (two soups)

Because we are contrarian nerds we decided (okay, I decided) to give the shortest chapter the longest chapter introduction. Let's talk about soup, okay? That might not sound like the best or most interesting way to begin a conversation or an introduction, but let's face it, soup is great. If there were a nation of Soup we would all want to go there, and often. In fact if there were a nation of Soup, I would be tempted to marry a resident of Soup Nation so that I could have dual citizenship and spend a lot of time in the nation of Soup without fear of deportation.

chilled melon and citrus soup with berry swirl

Yes, this soup is both cold and made of fruit. Now, before you go turning the page and second-guessing why you own this book, hear me out. It's not like there are a million recipes in this book, just a few. Just our best. If we could put only a few recipes in the book, would we put a gross one in? No, of course not. This recipe is light, refreshing, beautiful to look at, and makes me feel like a dainty lady every time I serve it. It is also perfect as a breakfast dish, or as the first course of a brunch or lunch.

Dainty ladies and dignified gents, your grocery list is as follows:

Melon and Citrus Soup

4 cups (2 melons' worth) of cantaloupe flesh (peeled and seeded, of course)

2 cups nectarine slices (no seeds, please)

1 cup orange slices (no seeds, please)

1½ cups vanilla soy yogurt (or plain or any fruity flavor)

4 tablespoons lemon juice

6 tablespoons maple syrup

1½ teaspoons finely minced mint leaves

Raspberry Puree

1 pint fresh, or 1 cup frozen, raspberries (or mixed berries)

2 tablespoons sugar (2½ tablespoons of sugar if using frozen berries)

2 tablespoons lime juice

To Make Soup

Puree all soup ingredients in a food processor until there are no chunks of anything. Refrigerate for at least 1 hour before serving, or if in a rush, put the soup in a shallow container, with the cover off, in the freezer for 20 minutes.

To Make the Puree

Blend all ingredients in a food processor until smooth. Pour the mixture into a small, fine mesh strainer and strain out all the raspberry seeds. Stirring the mixture helps to strain it quicker. Chill the puree until you are ready to serve the soup.

To Serve

Pour soup into individual bowls and swirl the puree in a nice design on top of the soup so you can feel extra dainty. Enjoy!

Makes 4 servings

I'm of the opinion that winter can be a bummer.

And unless you are a winter sport enthusiast or live in a place that doesn't ever get below 40 degrees, chances are you think winter can be a bummer too. But just the smell of this soup will make you forget all that snow you have to shovel before the sun goes down at 2:00 P.M.

What you will need in order to not want to fly south (or north if you are one of our friends in the Southern Hemisphere) for the winter:

3 tablespoons sesame oil

2 medium onions, chopped

1 tablespoon minced ginger root

4 garlic cloves, minced

2 tablespoons vegan margarine

¼ cup dry white wine

1 teaspoon salt

black pepper to taste

6 cups vegetable stock

1 cinnamon stick

2 whole cloves

4 fresh sage leaves

2 sprigs of thyme

1 small cheesecloth (You can buy these in the miscellaneous stuff aisle of any decent-sized grocery store—you know which aisle I'm talking about.)

2 pounds diced butternut squash

2 pears (any kind), diced

¼ cup silken tofu

Heat the oil in a large pot over medium-low heat. Stir in the onions, ginger root, and garlic and sauté for 5 minutes. Add the vegan margarine, wine, salt, and pepper, and sauté for 5 minutes more. Pour in the vegetable stock and turn the heat up to high.

Make a bouquet garni (fancy word for herb and spice goodies) of the cinnamon stick, cloves, sage, and thyme by tightly wrapping them in cheesecloth, and toss the bag into the pot. Once the mixture is almost boiling, add the squash and pears, turn the heat to low, and cook until the squash and pear pieces are really soft (about 40 minutes).

Turn off the heat, and take out the bouquet garni. Add the silken tofu, and stir mixture well. Puree half of the mixture in a food processor, then add back to the pot. Give the mixture a few good stirs, and it's ready to serve!

Makes 6 main course servings

the little idiot

In 1984, I worked at a record store in Darien, Connecticut, called Johnny's. Johnny's was far and away the most interesting place in Darien (apart from the Tory Hole Cave), as it was the only bastion of counterculturalism in an otherwise very conservative town. And one of the things that made Johnny's interesting was their practice of having an individual drawing on every bag that left the store. So when I started working at Johnny's, one of my jobs became drawing on the bags. The only problem was that I had never drawn before. My mother was an artist (specializing in a sort of loose figurative style) and as a result I had never really thought about drawing or painting because she was so good at it. And at a very early age, I had chosen to express myself creatively by playing music. But working at Johnny's involved drawing on bags, so I learned how to draw. Or to be more specific, I learned how to draw very simple little cartoon characters that were rudimentary at best.

I stopped working at Johnny's in 1985, but after I left, I still kept drawing my little cartoon characters. And then in the early nineties, I started making records and going on tour, and, on occasion, I found myself in the position of having to give an autograph to some deluded individual who thought that I was somehow important. It felt kind of cheap to just write my name on a piece of paper, so I started drawing cartoons in lieu of autographs. And then one day I was with a friend of mine and he referred to me as a "little idiot," and I laughed and laughed. (Because, well, it's true. I'm small and I'm kind of dim.) So seeing as my cartoon characters are quasi self-portraits, it just made sense to give them the name that my friend had given me, the Little Idiot. And the Little Idiot is originally from another planet (the location of which has yet to be discovered), which is also quasi autobiographical (what with me not being 100 percent human and whatnot).

—Moby

11

Chapter 11: The Booze-Fueled Romantic Nighttime Chapter

Teany is, by day, a bright and sunny and clean and happy place. But, at night, it becomes a veritable cesspool of depravity and degeneracy. Well, no, it doesn't. It's still a clean and happy place at night (although there are times when we wish that we owned a place that was a cesspool of depravity and degeneracy), although it does lend itself quite well to undepraved and undegenerate romance.

white sangria

This sangria

makes me dream about sitting on a porch and watching the sunset. Or maybe I have actually watched a beautiful sunset while sipping this delightful cocktail, and it just felt like a dream. Anyway, if you would like to get the kind of everything-is-going-to-be-okay feeling that only sangria can give you:

2 peaches or nectarines
2 pears
2 cups brandy
1 cup pure maple syrup
1 bottle of white wine (if you happen to have a few open bottles of white wine already, it's perfectly acceptable to mix them for sangria)
1 pint strawberries, sliced in quarters
1 pint blueberries (or raspberries or blackberries—whatever is in season)

Cut the peaches (or nectarines) and pears into bite-sized pieces. Marinate the fruit in the brandy and maple syrup for at least 6 hours, or for as long as 2 days.

In a large pitcher, combine the bottle of wine and half the marinated fruit along with half the marinade. Add half the strawberries and half the blueberries to the wine mix. Fill wine glasses or goblets with ice. Stir the sangria well and pour, being careful to evenly distribute the fruit to each glass. Serve the sangria with spoons so that whomever you're sharing your fuzzy sunset moment with can eagerly fish out more marinated fruit if they wish.

The other half of the marinated fruit—the strawberries and blueberries—is for the next pitcher of sangria you'll make after this one, because, speaking from experience, you won't want to stop at just one.

Makes ½ gallon

champagne mojito

10:20 P.M.: Order the following romantic food: Raspbellinis and vegan chocolate cheesecake.

10:45 P.M.: Order a couple of more Raspbellinis.

11:00 P.M.: Eh, what the hell, order a couple of more Raspbellinis. Notice how lovely your date looks in the soft, romantic candlelight.

11:15 P.M.: Pay your bill and tip your nice and conscientious teany waiter and walk arm in arm out of teany, having left the *Weekly World News* for someone else to enjoy. (It really is my favorite newspaper/magazine in the whole world. I mean, "Giant Ducks Guard the Gates of Hell" and "Osama and Saddam Adopt a Monkey Baby"? How much better can you get than that?)

11:30 P.M.: Wander aimlessly through the Lower East Side and the East Village, and if you're feeling adventurous, maybe go for a walk halfway across the Williamsburg Bridge and look at the beautiful Manhattan skyline in all of its shimmering glory.

12:30 A.M.: Wander back toward your date's apartment, maybe stopping for a nightcap at a quiet, romantic bar. Talk about your lives and your childhoods and funny things that happened when you were in junior high school and the worst kiss that you ever had when you were growing up. Notice how you miss your date when he/she goes to the bathroom, and how you perk up when you see her/him returning to your table.

1:15 A.M.: Walk your date home and tell him/her that you've had a wonderful time and kiss her/him on the sidewalk in front of his/her home. A nice kiss, not too long and not too crazy. Just a nice, romantic kiss. Then wander home feeling that warm suffusing glow that comes from having had a perfect date.

1:40 A.M.: Crawl into bed with a smile on your face and drift off to sleep thinking of the way that your date laughed at your jokes.

chocolate and green tea pudding

Like all

drug addictions, an addiction to chocolate is something that builds over time, wherein you always need a stronger quality and larger quantity of the drug in order to satisfy your addiction. Then one day you find yourself mainlining Baker's cocoa and desperately asking yourself, "Isn't there a more bitter-chocolate-creamy-kick-my-bum-and-satisfy-my-habit-for-good chocolatey treat out there?" I'd like to make an introduction: Fiending Chocoholic, say hello to teany's Chocolate and Green Tea Pudding.

> **1** cup chocolate soy milk
> **1** tablespoon loose green tea leaves
> **10** ounces (one bag) semisweet vegan chocolate chips
> **12** ounces silken tofu
> **¼** cup soft tofu
> **2** tablespoons matcha tea (green tea powder, available at any good tea shop or online), optional

Pour the chocolate milk and tea leaves into a small pot and bring to a boil. Turn off heat and let the chocolate milk cool. Melt the chocolate chips in a double boiler (or you can do this in a small pot over low heat, stirring constantly).

Put the soy milk mixture, melted chocolate, silken tofu, and soft tofu into a food processor. Blend until totally smooth. Put into individual cups or bowls, and refrigerate for at least 1 hour.

Before serving, take a paper doily or any other design cutout and lay it over the pudding.

(In the photograph, you will see that we've created a simple anarchy sign using three skewer sticks laid across the pudding to form the shape of an anarchy *A*.) Generously powder the top of the doily or cutout with the matcha. Lift the doily or cutout, making sure not to disturb the design you just made. Serve immediately.

Makes 5 servings

nighttime playlist

Doves—**The Last Broadcast**

Talking Heads—**Fear of Music**

Wire—**Chairs Missing**

Television—**Marquee Moon**

Brian Jonestown Massacre—**And This Is Our Music**

Clinic—**Walking with Thee**

Faith no More—**Who Cares a Lot? Greatest Hits**

Kraftwerk—**The Man Machine**

Julee Cruise—**Floating into the Night**

My Bloody Valentine—**Isn't Anything**

David Bowie—**Hunky Dory**

Ladytron—**604**

Television Personalities—
. . . And Don't the Kids Just Love It

Roxy Music—**Roxy Music**

Sometimes teany is really hectic and busy and lively at night, and other times it's sweet and quiet and dark and romantic. And because we want our customers to feel comfortable here, we wouldn't play a calming strings quartet album if the crowd was feeling frisky, and we wouldn't play a Judas Priest album if people were trying to be romantic (even though drinking tea to Judas Priest is actually pretty sexy). And we would never play Moby's music here, because that would just be weird. So this playlist isn't exactly a play-all-these-songs-together playlist, but more of a list of our nighttime favorites.

index

bios

Moby was born on September 11 (really), 1965 in Harlem, New York. He lived in Harlem until 1967, at which point he and his mother moved to Connecticut. Moby began playing music at the age of 8. Throughout his youth, Moby played in various punk rock bands and began dj'ing in 1984, after dropping out of college.

In 1990, Moby began releasing records. In the last 12 years, Moby has sold 15 million records and has earned gold, platinum, and multiplatinum records in more than 30 countries. Some of his career highlights have been:

1. writing and performing the closing music for the 2002 Winter Olympics for a televised audience of 2 billion people.

2. winning the world's bestselling alternative musician's award at the Monaco world music awards in 2001.

3. winning 4 MTV awards.

4. organizing and headlining the Area1 and Area2 concert festivals with performers such as David Bowie, Outkast, New Order, Paul Oakenfold, and many others. For more information please go to moby.com

Kelly was born on February 11, 1977 in Massachusetts. She grew up in Templeton, Mass., and began her higher education studying international politics in Boston in 1995. Kelly then moved to London, where she continued her studies at Regents College.

After returning to the United States she worked as a press writer at the White House in Clinton's administration. Kelly graduated in 1999 with a degree in international politics from Suffolk University, Boston.

In 2000 Kelly moved to New York City and worked at Human Rights Watch before starting teany.

Little idiot bio

hi.